CHIC KNITS
Stylish Designs from KNITPORT

Phuong My Ly

Martingale®
& COMPANY

CREDITS

President & CEO: Tom Wierzbicki
Publisher: Jane Hamada
Editorial Director: Mary V. Green
Managing Editor: Tina Cook
Technical Editor: Donna Druchunas
Copy Editor: Sheila Chapman Ryan
Design Director: Stan Green
Production Manager: Regina Girard
Illustrator: Adrienne Smitke
Cover & Text Designer: Shelly Garrison
Photographer: Brent Kane

Chic Knits:
Stylish Designs from Knitport
© 2008 by Phuong My Ly

Martingale®
& COMPANY

Martingale & Company
20205 144th Ave. NE
Woodinville, WA 98072-8478 USA
www.martingale-pub.com

Printed in China

13 12 11 10 09 08   8 7 6 5 4 3 2 1

Library of Congress Cataloging-in-Publication Data
Library of Congress Control Number: 2007045976

ISBN: 978-1-56477-826-0

MISSION STATEMENT

Dedicated to providing quality products and service to inspire creativity.

DEDICATION
For my children and grandchildren

ACKNOWLEDGMENTS

I would like to send a heartfelt thank-you to all my customers and students for their support these past few years. Special thanks to Debi Lewis, Karen Levine, My Hoa Hertler, Rhonda Stevenson, Sheila Sparr, and Tina Lavendier for contributing their efforts.

Thanks to the lovely models Ashley Wong, Becky Vollbrecht, Brenda Huynh, Emma Murphy, Megan Sweasey, and Melia Nordquist. The silver and crystal beaded jewelry was designed by Brenda Huynh.

I would like to thank everyone at Martingale & Company for making *Chic Knits* possible. Special thanks to Mary, Karen, Stan, Brent, Shelly, Tina, Tami, and Donna for their patience and hard work.

My biggest thank-you goes to my two precious daughters, Brittany and Brenda, for their inspiration and effort in putting this book together.

And last but not least, many thanks to my husband, Man X. Huynh, for his unwavering support in anything I do.

CONTENTS

Introduction

When I learned my first grandchild was expected, I created a line of baby knits for him. From this beginning grew numerous lines of unique and practical knitwear, and eventually a knitting boutique called Knitport.

As a sculptor, I believe that knitting is an art, like sculpting. Each fiber of yarn is an opportunity to express yourself, no matter how structured the knitting pattern you're working from. Needles are like fingers that mold or tools that carve. Colors are like emotions embedded in threads lovingly woven. Life is the inspiration for each yarn sculpture.

In this book, each piece is an expression of life and love. Every design is wearable, practical, and chic. Every pattern keeps the beginner in mind with simple, easy-to-understand diagrams and instructions.

More than two years after my boutique opened its doors, students gather at Knitport to be inspired and to learn. Knitport, located in Thousand Oaks, California, offers service and craftsmanship in a setting that is tranquil, modern, and inspiring. In this book, I would like you to have the same Knitport experience, even if you can't visit California. In these pages, I've included a selection of projects for knitters of all skill levels. For those who want to expand their skills or who need help with the techniques in the patterns, I've also included a chapter on my favorite knitting tips and techniques. As you explore these pages and try your hand at some of the projects and techniques, I encourage you to let your creativity flow and to make your unique knitting pieces an expression of your own life and love.

my needles land at

Knitport
™

SUMMER ALLURE SHELL

TEASER WRAP

TIFFANY CARDIGAN

JULIA AND HAZEL BAGS

ITSY-BITSY BIKINI

PASSION SWEATER

HONEY SHRUG

15

KAREN BAG

CUDDLE WRAP

MYSTIQUE CAPE

BOYFRIEND SCARF

BOYFRIEND SWEATER

HAZEL BAG

FELTED FLOWERS

SUMMER ALLURE SHELL

This alluring shell will entice and flatter, whether it's worn at the office under a blazer or at night out on the town. A simple knit pattern for the body contrasts with a lacy pattern on top, creating an intricate look that is actually easy to make.

SIZES

This top has negative ease, which means the sweater measurement is smaller than body size, for a body-hugging fit.

To fit bust: 32–34 (34–36, 36–38)"

Finished bust measurements: 24 (26½, 29½)"

Finished length (including straps): 22½ (23, 23½)"

SKILL LEVEL: INTERMEDIATE

MATERIALS

3 (4, 5) skeins of Brilla from Filatura di Crosa (42% cotton, 58% rayon; 1.75 oz/50 g; 120 yds/110 m) in color 412 (plum) ⓸

Size 8 and 9 needles or sizes required to obtain gauge

Size 10 needles for BO

Size D-3 (3.25 mm) crochet hook

Stitch markers

Tapestry needle

GAUGE

17 sts and 26 rows = 4" in St st on size 9 needles

19 sts and 28 rows = 4" in St st on size 8 needles

NOTE: Don't work any special selvage stitches. Work the edge stitches in stockinette stitch as for the rest of the row.

BACK

With size 9 needles, CO 52 (58, 64) sts.

Row 1 (WS): P13 (15, 17), pm, P26 (28, 30), pm, purl to end.

Row 2 (RS): Knit.

Work even in St st for 31 rows.

Row 34 (RS): Knit to 2 sts before first marker, K2tog, sm, knit to next marker, sm, skp, knit to end—50 (56, 62) sts rem.

Work in St st for 5 rows.

Row 40 (RS): Rep row 34—48 (54, 60) sts rem.

Work in St st for 5 rows.

Row 46 (RS): Rep row 34—46 (52, 58) sts rem.

Knit onto size 8 needles and work even in St st for 19 rows. Change back to size 9 needles.

Row 66 (RS): Knit to marker, M1, sm, knit to next marker, sm, M1, knit to end—48 (54, 60) sts.

Work in St st for 5 rows.

Row 72 (RS): Rep row 66—50 (56, 62) sts.

Work in St st for 5 rows.

Row 78 (RS): Rep row 66—52 (58, 64) sts.

Remove markers.

Work in St st for 19 rows or until body measures approx 15½" from beg. End after completing a WS row.

SHAPE ARMHOLE:

BO 4 (4, 5) sts at beg of next 2 rows—44 (50, 54) sts rem.

BO 2 (3, 3) sts at beg of next 2 rows—40 (44, 48) sts rem.

Row 102 (RS): K1, skp, knit until 3 sts rem, K2tog, K1—38 (42, 46) sts rem.

Row 103 (WS): Purl.

LACE PATT:

Row 104 (RS): K1, *K2tog, YO; rep from * to last 3 sts, K2tog, K1—37 (41, 45) sts rem.

Row 105 (WS): K1, *K2tog, YO; rep from * to last 2 sts, K2—37 (41, 45) sts.

Work row 105 another 19 (21, 23) times. End after completing a RS row.

BO kw with size 10 needles, insert crochet hook in last lp of BO and ch st for 6 (7, 8)" to make shoulder strap. Cut yarn, leaving 6"-long tail for finishing.

FRONT

With size 9 needle, CO 52 (58, 64) sts.

Work same as back to row 103.

Work even in St st for 6 rows.

LACE PATT:

Row 110 (RS): K1, *K2tog, YO; rep from * to last 3 sts, K2tog, K1—37 (41, 45) sts rem.

Row 111 (WS): K1, *K2tog, YO; rep from * to last 2 sts, K2.

Work row 111 another 13 (15, 17) times. End after completing a RS row.

BO kw with size 10 needle, insert crochet hook in last lp of BO and ch st for 6 (7, 8)" to make shoulder strap. Cut yarn, leaving 6"-long tail for finishing.

FINISHING

Using mattress st, sew side seams.

Front shoulder strap: Pull ch strap from point A to point B through corner of back piece, and then through corner of front piece. Tie 3 times to secure and weave in end.

Back shoulder strap: Work as for front strap, bringing ch strap from point C to point D through corner of front piece, and then through corner of back piece. Tie 3 times to secure and weave in end.

Choose a color that suits your style and taste. This version was knit in Brilla from Filatura di Crosa in color 408.

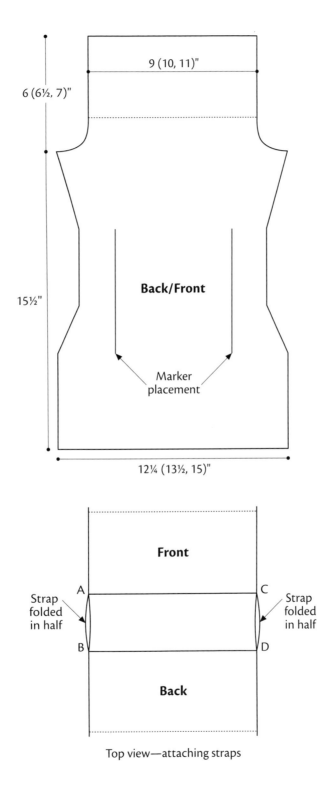

9 (10, 11)"

6 (6½, 7)"

Back/Front

15½"

Marker
placement

12¼ (13½, 15)"

Front

A   C

Strap
folded
in half

Strap
folded
in half

B   D

Back

Top view—attaching straps

TEASER WRAP

Wear this wrap
with jeans or wear
it with a dress. The
drop stitch combined
with a metallic fiber
makes for a sassy,
shimmering look.

SIZE

Approx 12" unstretched; approx 16" x 65" as worn

SKILL LEVEL: EASY

MATERIALS

6 skeins of Gatsby from Katia (77% viscose, 15% nylon, 8% polyester; 1.75 oz/ 50 g; 129 yds/118 m) in color 20 (gold) 2

Size 9 needles or size required to obtain gauge

Size E-4 (3.5 mm) crochet hook

Tapestry needle

Sewing needle and matching thread

GAUGE

Approx 21 sts = 4" in garter st unstretched

NOTE: Slip the first stitch of every row for a neat, tidy selvage.

SPECIAL STITCHES

Elongated st: K1, wrapping the yarn around needle twice instead of once

(Note that if you K1 and **then** wrap twice, the stitch will be too long when you drop it.)

WRAP

CO 64 sts.

Row 1: Sl 1 kw, K1, *YO, K2tog; rep from * to last 2 sts, K2.

Rows 2–4: Knit.

Row 5: Sl 1 kw, *work 1 elongated st; rep from * to last st, K1.

Row 6: Sl 1 kw, knit across, dropping all extra wraps.

Rows 7–9: Knit.

Rep rows 1–9 until the wrap is the desired length without fringe, or you have used up 5 skeins of yarn.

BO kw.

Cut 80 pieces of yarn 15" long. Using 2 strands for each fringe, use the crochet hook to attach 20 fringes evenly spaced across each end of shawl. (See "Making Fringe" on page 75.)

TIFFANY CARDIGAN

Add sophistication and elegance to any outfit with this cardigan. The texture and shape create a structured and flattering appearance. This look is accomplished with simple knit and purl stitches and a refined summer yarn.

SIZES

This top has negative ease, which means the sweater measurement is smaller than body size, for a body-hugging fit.

To fit bust: 32–34 (34–36, 36–38, 38–40, 40–42)"

Finished bust measurement: 30 (32, 34, 36, 38)"

Sweater length: 17 (17½, 18, 19, 19½)"

Sleeve length: 15 (15¼, 16, 17, 17½)"

SKILL LEVEL: INTERMEDIATE

MATERIALS

9 (10, 11, 12, 13) skeins of Glisten from Louisa Harding (97% nylon, 3% polyester; 1.75 oz/50 g; 93 yds/85 m) in color 3 (aqua)

Size 9 circular needle (24") or size required to obtain gauge

Size 8 circular needle (24")

Size 8 circular needle (35") for front bands

Tapestry needle

4 buttons, ¾" diameter

Sewing needle and matching thread

GAUGE

20 sts and 28 rows = 4" in St st on size 9 needle

NOTE: Don't work any special selvage stitches. Work the edge stitches in stockinette stitch as for the rest of the row.

BACK

With 24" smaller needle, CO 62 (68, 74, 80, 86) sts.

Row 1 (WS): *K1, P1; rep from * to end.

Row 2 (RS): Rep row 1.

Work ribbing for 9 more rows or until piece measures 1¾" from beg. End after completing a WS row. Change to larger needle.

Row 12 (RS): Knit.

Row 13 (WS): Purl.

Work in St st for 10 rows or until piece measures 3½" from beg. End after completing a WS row.

Row 24 (RS): K1, M1, knit to last st, M1, K1—64 (70, 76, 82, 88) sts.

Work 5 (5, 5, 7, 7) rows even in St st.

Work row 24 every 6 (6, 6, 8, 8) rows another 5 times—74 (80, 86, 92, 98) sts.

Work even until piece measures 10½ (10½, 11, 11½, 11½)" from beg. End after completing a WS row.

SHAPE ARMHOLES:

BO 3 (3, 4, 5, 5) sts at beg of next 2 rows—68 (74, 78, 82, 88) sts rem.

BO 1 (2, 2, 3, 3) sts at beg of next 2 rows—66 (70, 74, 76, 82) sts rem.

Next row (RS): K1, skp, knit to last 3 sts, K2tog, K1—64 (68, 72, 74, 80) sts rem.

Next row (WS): Purl.

Work last 2 rows another 0 (1, 1, 0, 2) times—64 (66, 70, 74, 76) sts rem.

Work even in St st until armholes measure 6 (6 1/4, 6½, 7, 7½)". End after completing a WS row.

SHAPE SHOULDERS:

BO shoulders loosely as follows:

Next row (RS): BO 10 (10, 10, 11, 11) sts kw at beg of row, knit to end.

Next row (WS): BO 10 (10, 10, 11, 11) sts pw at beg of row, purl to end.

Next row (RS): BO kw 10 (10, 11, 11, 11) sts kw at beg of row, knit to end.

Next row (WS): BO pw 10 (10, 11, 11, 11) sts pw at beg of row, purl to end—24 (26, 28, 30, 32) sts rem.

BO rem sts loosely.

RIGHT FRONT

With 24" smaller needle, CO 31 (34, 37, 40, 43) sts.

Work same as back for 23 rows or until piece measures 3½" from beg. End after completing a WS row.

Row 24 (RS): Knit to last st, M1, K1—32 (35, 38, 41, 44) sts.

Work 5 (5, 5, 7, 7) rows even.

Work row 24 every 6 (6, 6, 8, 8) rows another 5 times—37 (40, 43, 46, 49) sts.

Work even until piece measures 8 (8, 8½, 9, 9)" from beg. End after completing a WS row.

SHAPE V-NECK AND ARMHOLE:

Row 1 (RS): K2, skp, knit to end—36 (39, 42, 45, 48) sts rem.

Rows 2–4: Work even in St st.

Rows 5–16: Work rows 1–4 another 3 times—33 (36, 39, 42, 45) sts rem.

Row 17: K2, skp, knit to end—32 (35, 38, 41, 44) sts rem.

Row 18 (WS): BO 3 (3, 4, 5, 5) sts,

purl to end—29 (32, 34, 36, 39) sts rem.

Row 19: Knit.

Row 20 (WS): BO 1 (2, 2, 3, 3) st, purl to end—28 (30, 32, 33, 36) sts rem.

Row 21: K2, skp, knit to last 2 sts, K2tog—26 (28, 30, 31, 34) sts rem.

Row 22: Purl.

Cont to dec 1 st at armhole another 0 (1, 1, 0, 2) times. AT THE SAME TIME, dec at neck edge every 4 rows until 20 (20, 21, 22, 22) sts rem.

Work even until armhole measures 6 (6 1/4, 6½, 7, 7½)". End after completing a RS row.

SHAPE SHOULDERS:

BO loosely as follows:

Next row (WS): BO 10 (10, 10, 11, 11) sts, purl to end—10 (10, 11, 11, 11) sts rem.

Next row (RS): Knit.

On WS, BO rem sts loosely. Cut yarn, leaving an 18" tail for sewing.

LEFT FRONT

With 24" smaller needle, CO 31 (34, 37, 40, 43) sts.

Work same as back for 23 rows or until piece measures 3½" from beg. End after completing a WS row.

Row 24 (RS): K1, M1, knit to end—32 (35, 38, 41, 44) sts.

Work 5 (5, 5, 7, 7) rows even.

Work row 24 every 6 (6, 6, 8, 8) rows another 5 times—37 (40, 43, 46, 49) sts.

Work even until piece measures 8 (8, 8 ½, 9, 9)" from beg. End after completing a WS row.

SHAPE V-NECK AND ARMHOLE:

Row 1 (RS): Knit to last 4 sts, K2tog, K2—36 (39, 42, 45, 48) sts rem.

Rows 2–4: Work even in St st.

Rows 5–16: Rep rows 1–4 another 3 times—33 (36, 39, 42, 45) sts rem.

Row 17: BO 3 (3, 4, 5, 5) sts, knit to last 4 sts, K2tog, K2—29 (32, 34, 36, 39) sts rem.

Row 18: Purl.

Row 19: BO 1 (2, 2, 3, 3) sts, knit to end—28 (30, 32, 33, 36) sts rem.

Row 20: Purl.

Row 21 (RS): K1, skp, knit to last 4 sts, K2tog, K2—26 (28, 30, 31, 34) sts rem.

Cont to dec 1 st at armhole another 0 (1, 1, 0, 2) times. AT THE SAME TIME, dec at neck edge every 4 rows until 20 (20, 21, 22, 22) sts rem.

Work even until armhole measures 6 (6 1/4, 6½, 7, 7½)". End after completing a WS row.

SHAPE SHOULDERS:

BO loosely as follows:

Next row (RS): BO 10 (10, 10, 11, 11) sts, knit to end—10 (10, 11, 11, 11) sts rem.

Next row (WS): Purl.

BO rem sts loosely. Cut yarn, leaving an 18" tail for sewing.

SLEEVES (MAKE 2)

With 24" smaller needle, CO 46 (48, 50, 52, 54) sts.

Row 1 (WS): *K1, P1; rep from * to end of row.

Row 2 (RS): Rep row 1.

Work ribbing as established for 13 rows or until piece measures 2" from beg. End after completing a WS row. Change to larger needle.

Row 14 (RS): Knit.

Row 15: Purl.

Work even in St st for another 6 rows.

Row 22 (RS): K1, M1, knit to last st, M1, K1—48 (50, 52, 54, 56) sts.

Work even in St st for 7 rows.

Work row 22 every 8 rows another 5 (5, 5, 6, 6) times—58 (60, 62, 66, 68) sts.

Work even until piece measures 10½ (10½, 11, 11½, 11½)" from beg. End after completing a WS row.

SHAPE SLEEVE CAPS:

BO 6 (6, 7, 7, 7) sts at beg of next 2 rows—46 (48, 48, 52, 54) sts rem.

Next row (RS): K1, skp, knit to last 3 sts, K2tog, K1—44 (46, 46, 50, 52) sts rem.

Next row: Purl.

Work dec row every knit row another 4 times—36 (38, 38, 42, 44) sts rem.

Work even for 3 (3, 5, 5, 7) rows. End after completing a WS row.

Next row (RS): K1, skp, knit to last 3 sts, K2tog, K1—34 (36, 36, 40, 42) sts rem.

Next row: Purl.

Work last 2 rows another 3 (3, 4, 4, 5) times—28 (30, 28, 32, 32) sts rem.

BO 2 sts at beg of next 2 rows—24 (26, 24, 28, 28) sts rem.

BO 3 (3, 3, 4, 4) sts at beg of next 2 rows—18 (20, 18, 20, 20) sts rem.

BO all sts tightly.

FINISHING

Using mattress st, sew shoulder, side, and sleeve seams. Center sleeve to shoulder seams and use mattress st to sew sleeves into armholes.

BUTTON BAND:

With RS of right front facing you, connect new ball of yarn. Using 35" size 8 circular needle, PU 104 (104, 108, 112, 112) sts evenly along right front, PU 24 (26, 28, 30, 32) sts across back of neck, and 103 (103, 107, 111, 111) sts evenly along left front—231 (233, 243, 253, 255) sts total.

Row 1 (WS): P2, K1, *P1, K1; rep from * to last 2 sts, P2.

Row 2 (RS): K2, P1, *K1, P1; rep from * to last 2 sts, K2.

Work 1 row in ribbing as established.

BUTTON HOLE:

Row 4 (RS): Work 4 sts in ribbing, *YO, K2tog, work 16 (16, 18, 20, 20) sts in ribbing*; rep from * to * 3 times, work ribbing to end.

Cont in ribbing, working YO sts into patt as established, for 4 more rows.

BO in patt with larger needle.

Sew on buttons.

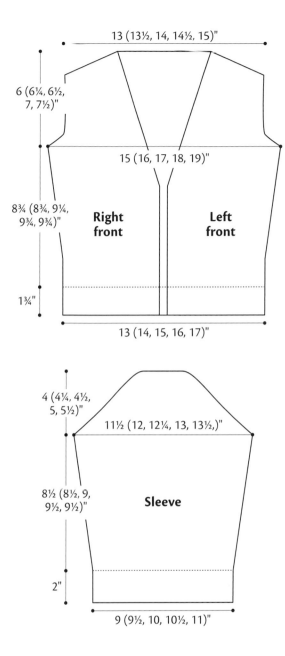

13 (13½, 14, 14½, 15)"

6 (6¼, 6½, 7, 7½)"

15 (16, 17, 18, 19)"

8¾ (8¾, 9¼, 9¾, 9¾)"

Right front   **Left front**

1¾"

13 (14, 15, 16, 17)"

4 (4¼, 4½, 5, 5½)"

11½ (12, 12¼, 13, 13½,)"

8½ (8½, 9, 9½, 9½)"

Sleeve

2"

9 (9½, 10, 10½, 11)"

JULIA BAG

This bag will turn heads everywhere you go. Created with a simple knit stitch and a circular needle, this design allows you to add your own twist by attaching silk or felted flowers.

SIZES

The size is based on your tension and the felting process. The bag shown on page 34 is the large size.

Medium (Large)

Before felting: Approx 24 (26)" tall x 44 (50)" in circumference

After felting: Approx 11 (13)" tall x 26 (32)" in circumference

SKILL LEVEL: INTERMEDIATE

MATERIALS

NOTE: Either Nature Wool or Nature Wool Chunky can be used for this project, giving you more color choices. Both yarn weights work well for felting. Nature Wool is thinner, so use 3 strands of yarn held together to knit with. Nature Wool Chunky is thicker, so you only need 2 strands of yarn held together.

MC 5 (6) skeins of Nature Wool from Araucania (100% wool; 3.52 oz/100 g; 240 yds/220 m) in 107 (olive)

or

MC 5 (6) skeins of Nature Wool Chunky from Araucania (100% wool; 3.52 oz/100 g; 132 yds/120 m) in color 114 (tan)

CC 1 skein of Linie 85 Smash from Online (100% polyester; 1.75 oz/50 g; 99 yds/90 m) in color 0010 (tan)

Size 17 circular needle (35") or size required to obtain gauge

Tapestry needle

Sharp darning needle

1 pair of purse handles, 20" long

3 purchased silk flowers in different sizes (or make your own flowers following the instructions on page 70)

Scrubbing brush

GAUGE

Gauge is not important here. Loose is better than tight. If you knit too tightly, the pieces may not felt properly. Use 2 strands of Nature Wool Chunky or 3 strands of Nature Wool held together to make a swatch.

BOTTOM

Using 2 strands of Nature Wool Chunky or 3 strands of Nature Wool, CO 32 (36) sts with MC.

Knit every row for 24 (28) rows. Do not BO. PU 11 (13) sts on short side, PU 32 (36) sts on long side, and then PU 11 (13) sts on short side—86 (98) sts total. (See diagram.)

BODY OF BAG:

Knit in the round until piece measures 20 (22)" from PU.

Cut 1 strand of MC and **add** 1 strand of CC. Work in the round until piece measures 4" from adding CC.

BO loosely.

FINISHING

Fold top 2" down to the inside and use 2 strands of MC to whipstitch all around. Weave in ends. Use scrubbing brush to brush out CC section until it is full of long eyelash. Felt the bag according to the instructions on page 76.

SHAPING BAG:

Shape, mold, and sculpt your bag until you are happy with it. Stuff bag with tissue paper. Cut cardboard to fit bottom of bag and place it inside to keep the shape as it dries.

ATTACH HANDLES:

Thread sharp darning needle with 1 strand of MC and double it so you are sewing with 2 strands of yarn.

Place handle on bag using diagram as guide. Sew in and out from point A to point B. Make sure to secure and weave in tail. Repeat on other side of bag to attach 2nd handle.

ATTACH FLOWERS:

Sew purchased or felted flowers (see page 70 to make your own) to the bag using the photo and your imagination as a guide.

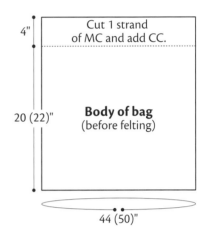

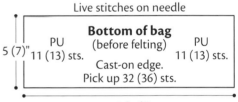

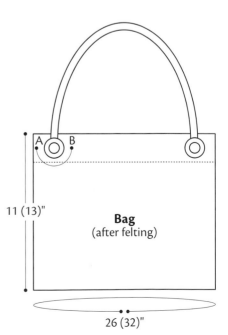

CHARM SHRUG

The perfect
accessory to any
outfit, this design
is made to mold to
the body. Slip, knit,
and purl are the
primary techniques;
these stitches and
the textured yarn
create a ruffled
effect at the edge
of the shrug.

SIZES

To fit bust: 32–34 (34–36, 36–38)"

Finished bust measurements: 29½ (32, 34½)"

Length: 16 (17, 18)"

SKILL LEVEL: EXPERIENCED

MATERIALS

5 (6, 6) skeins of Monte Carlo from Queensland Collection (61% cotton, 36% viscose, 3% polyester; 1.75 oz/50 g; 99 yds/90 m) in color 5 (variegated tans) [4]

2 size 7 circular needles (16" and 24") or size required to obtain gauge

Tapestry needle

2 stitch holders

8 stitch markers (4 red and 4 blue, or use the colors of your choice)

GAUGE

18 sts and 23 rows = 4" in St st

NOTE: Slip the first stitch of every row for a neat, tidy selvage.

SPECIAL STITCHES

Raglan shaping: YO before each blue marker and after each red marker, every RS row. Always have 1 st between the 2 markers.

BODY

This pattern is knitted from neck down.

UPPER BODY AND SHOULDERS:

With longer needle, CO 44 (50, 56) sts.

Row 1 (WS): P10 (12, 14), pm (red), P1, pm (blue), P22 (24, 26), pm (red), P1, pm (blue), P10 (12, 14)—44 (50, 56) sts.

Row 2 (RS): Sl 1 kw, K1, M1, knit to marker, YO, sm, K1, sm, YO, knit to marker, YO, sm, K1, sm, YO, K8 (10, 12), M1, K2—50 (56, 62) sts.

Row 3 (WS): Sl 1 pw, purl.

Row 4 (RS): Sl 1 kw, K1, pm (blue), K1, pm (red), knit to marker, YO, sm, K1, sm, YO, knit to marker, YO, sm, K1, sm, YO, knit until 3 sts rem, pm (blue), K1, pm (red), K2—54 (60, 66) sts.

Row 5 (WS): Sl 1 pw, purl.

Row 6 (RS): Sl 1 kw, K1, M1, YO, sm, K1, sm, YO, knit to marker, YO, sm, K1, sm, YO, knit to marker, YO, sm, K1, sm, YO, knit to marker, YO, sm, K1, sm, YO, M1, K2—64 (70, 76) sts.

Row 7 (WS): Sl 1 pw, purl.

Row 8 (RS): Sl 1 kw, knit to marker, YO, sm, K1, sm, YO, knit to marker, YO, sm, K1, sm, YO, knit to marker, YO, sm, K1, sm, YO, knit to marker, YO, sm, K1, sm, YO, K4—72 (78, 84) sts.

Row 9 (WS): Sl 1 pw, purl.

Row 10 (RS): Sl 1 kw, K1, M1, knit to marker, YO, sm, K1, sm, YO, knit to marker, YO, sm, K1, sm, YO, knit to marker, YO, sm, K1, sm, YO, knit to marker, YO, sm, K1, sm, YO, knit to last 2 sts, M1, K2—82 (88, 94) sts.

Row 11 (WS): Sl 1 pw, purl.

Work rows 8–11 another 8 (9, 10) times, then work rows 8 and 9 once more—234 (258, 282) sts.

Work 5 rows without YO at markers, but cont to M1 2 sts after beg of rows and before last 2 sts at the end of rows every 4 rows as above. End after completing a WS row.

SHAPE LOWER BODY:

Next row (RS): Knit to blue marker, remove marker, K1, remove red marker, transfer 51 (58, 64) sts up to blue marker to stitch holder for sleeve, remove blue marker, K1, remove red marker, knit to blue marker, remove blue marker, K1, remove red marker, transfer 51 (58, 64) sts up to blue marker to stitch holder for sleeve, remove blue marker, K1, remove red marker, knit to end—130 (142, 154) sts for body.

Next row (RS): K2, M1, knit to last 2 sts, M1, K2.

Next row (WS): Purl.

Work last 2 rows another 4 times. End after completing a WS row.

Continue working back and forth in St st, M1 after first 2 sts and before last 2 sts every 4 rows, until back measures 15 (16, 17)" long from neck. End after completing a WS row.

MAKE RUFFLE:

Row 1 (RS): CO 2 sts at beg of row, *K1, M1; rep from * to last st, K1.

Rows 2 and 4: CO 2 sts at beg of row, purl to end.

Row 3: CO 2 sts at beg of row, knit to end.

BO all sts loosely.

SLEEVES

Work one sleeve at a time.

With RS facing you, transfer all sts from st holder for 1 sleeve onto shorter circular needle and tie on yarn. Do not join to knit in the round.

Row 1 (RS): Knit.

Row 2 (WS): Purl.

Cont working in St st for 2" and dec 1 st at each end every 4 rows 4 times—43 (50, 56) sts remain. Work even until sleeve measures 5" long from armhole. End after completing a WS row.

Next Row (RS): *K1, M1; rep from * to last st, K1.

Work 3 rows even.

BO loosely.

Repeat for 2nd sleeve.

FINISHING

Using mattress st, sew sleeve seams.

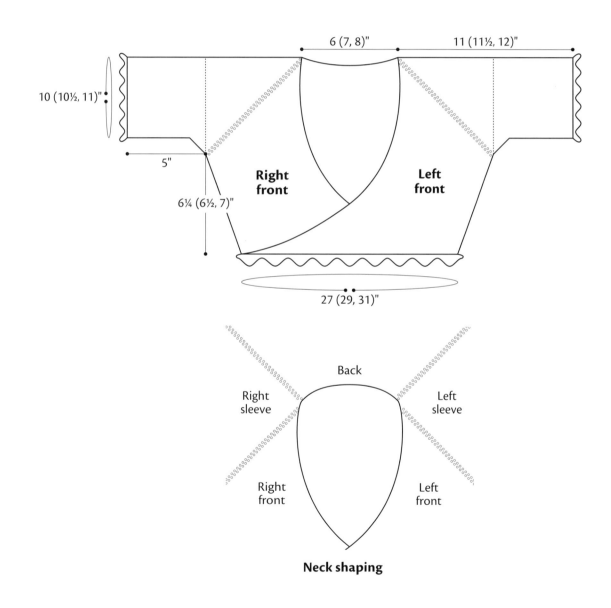

Neck shaping

Itsy-Bitsy Bikini

This sexy look makes for a bold but tasteful appearance on the beach. Wear it with a skirt and show off on the sidewalks of Palm Beach.

SIZES

This bikini has the top and bottom sized separately so you can choose the exact sizes to fit your figure. The top is sized according to bra cup size and the bottom is sized according to your hip measurement. Both pieces tie on, providing a flexible fit.

To fit bust: A (B, C, D) cup; adjust to fit around ribcage with ties

To fit hips: 32–34 (34–36, 36–38, 38–40)"; adjust to fit around hips with ties

SKILL LEVEL: INTERMEDIATE

MATERIALS

5 (6, 7, 7) skeins of Velour from Muench (100% nylon; .87 oz/25 g; 63 yds/58 m) in color 10 (hot pink)

Size 3 needles or size required to obtain gauge

Size 8 needles to BO

Size C-2 (2.75 mm) crochet hook

Tapestry needle

Small seashells with predrilled holes

Safety pins

GAUGE

24 sts and 37 rows = 4" in St st on size 3 needles

NOTE: Don't work any special selvage stitches. Work the edge stitches in stockinette stitch as for the rest of the row.

CUP (MAKE 2)

CO 36 (40, 44, 48) sts on size 3 needles.

MAKE CASING:

Row 1 (WS): Purl.

Row 2: Knit.

Work 9 rows even in St st for casing.

SHAPE CUP:

Row 12 (RS): K2, K2tog tbl, knit until 4 sts remain, K2tog, K2—34 (38, 42, 46) sts rem.

Rows 13–15: Work even in St st.

Work last 4 rows another 0 (2, 3, 4) times—34 (34, 36, 38) sts rem.

Cont to dec as in row 12 every RS row until 4 sts rem.

Do not BO.

WORK CROCHET TIE:

Cut yarn, leaving 38 (40, 43, 45)" tail. Pull tail through all 4 sts with crochet hook or tapestry needle.

With RS facing you, sc, working tight sts, along right side of triangle from the bottom up (see diagram on page 77). Cut yarn, leaving 35 (35, 40, 40)" tail. Pull tail through all 4 sts.

With a separate piece of yarn, connect yarn from top, leaving 35 (35, 40, 40)" tail and pull through 4 sts. With RS facing you, sc, working tight sts, down left side of triangle.

Cut 3 strands 70 (70, 80, 80)" long, and pull strands halfway through all 4 sts, creating 6 strands that are 35 (35, 40, 40)" long.

You should now have a total of 9 strands running through the 4 sts at top of cup. Divide strands into 3 groups and braid them very tightly together. Tie a knot, leaving 4" tail and trim ends evenly if desired. Repeat for 2nd casing.

Finishing Top

Cut 12 strands of yarn, each 75 (80, 85, 90)" long. Tie knot on 1 end, leaving 5" tails. Divide yarn into 3 sections and braid very tightly, then tie knot at end of braid, leaving 5" tails.

Place cups on flat surface with WS facing up, then place braid along bottom edge of both cups. Fold up casing and backstitch in place over braid (see diagram on page 41).

ATTACH SEASHELLS:

Pull a strand of yarn at end of braid through a seashell and knot to secure shell. Repeat as many times as you want to embellish your bikini with seashells.

Tie bikini top to fit.

BOTTOM

CO 66 (72, 78, 84) sts on size 3 needles.

BACK:

Row 1 (WS): Purl.

Row 2 (RS): Knit.

Work in St st for 9 more rows, end after completing a WS row.

Row 12 (RS): K2, K2tog tbl, knit to last 4 sts, K2tog, K2—64 (70, 76, 82) sts rem.

Row 13: Purl.

Row 14: Knit.

Row 15: Purl.

Work last 4 rows another 2 (3, 4, 5) times—60 (64, 68, 72) sts rem.

Cont to dec alternating between every 4 rows and every 2 rows until you have worked another 15 (15, 17, 17) decrease rows—30 (34, 34, 38) sts rem. End after completing a WS row.

Work 3 rows even.

Work row 12 every RS row a total of 9 (11, 10, 11) times—12 (12, 14, 16) sts rem.

Work even for 12 (12, 14, 16) rows. End after completing a WS row.

FRONT:

Next row (RS): K2, M1, knit to last 2 sts, M1, K2—14 (14, 16, 18) sts.

Work 3 rows even.

Cont to M1 every 4 rows another 3 (3, 4, 5) times —20 (20, 24, 28) sts. End after completing a WS row.

Cont to M1 every 3 rows a total of 4 (4, 6, 6) times—28 (28, 36, 40) sts. End after completing a WS row.

Cont to M1 every RS row a total of 11 (14, 13, 14) times—50 (56, 62, 68) sts. End after completing a RS row.

CO 1 st at beg of next 6 rows—56 (62, 68, 74) sts.

Work even for 3 rows.

BO using size 8 needles.

Finishing Bottom

CROCHET TRIM ON LEG OPENINGS:

With RS facing you and starting at point A (see diagram at right), work hdc along back bottom, making tight sts, then work hdc to front bottom with normal tension to point B, cut yarn. Weave in tail.

With RS facing you and starting at point C, work hdc from front bottom with normal tension and hdc to back bottom, working tightly to point D. Cut yarn and weave in tail.

FRONT TIE:

Cut 12 strands of yarn, each 42 (46, 50, 54)" long. Knot 1 end, leaving 4" tails. Divide yarn into 3 sections and braid very tightly until 5" tails remain, then put safety pins into all tails. Weave braid in and out of fabric, 1" apart, along front of bottom from B to C. Pull braid through evenly and tie a knot, leaving 4" tails. Trim ends evenly if desired.

BACK TIE:

Cut 12 strands of yarn, each 50 (52, 56, 60)" long. Repeat as for front tie along back of bottom from A to D.

Attach seashells to ties as for top.

Tie bikini on both sides to fit.

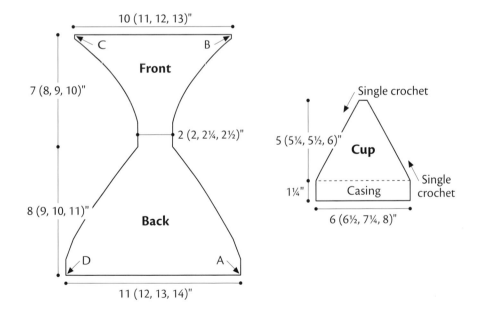

PASSION SWEATER

This sweater will keep you warm in winter without any bulk. Use a bold color such as red and this simple knit-and-purl creation will be a classic item in your closet for years to come.

SIZES

Sweater is loosely knitted. It will stretch to fit bust indicated below.

To fit bust: 32–34 (34–36, 36–38, 38–40)"

Finished bust measurement: 28¾ (31, 33½, 35¾)"

Length (excluding cowl): 20½ (21½, 23, 24)"

SKILL LEVEL: INTERMEDIATE

MATERIALS

4 (4, 5, 5) skeins of Gioiello from Filatura di Crosa (30% kid mohair, 30% wool, 20% nylon, 10% cotton, 10% acrylic; 1.75 oz/50 g; 220 yds/200 m) in color 5 (red) 🧶 4

Size 9 circular needle (24") or size required to obtain gauge

Size 8 circular needle (24")

Size 10½ needles to BO

Size E-4 (3.5 mm) crochet hook

Tapestry needle and stitch markers

GAUGE

17 sts and 24 rows = 4" in St st on size 9 needle

NOTE: Don't work any special selvage stitches. Work the edge stitches in stockinette stitch as for the rest of the row.

BACK AND FRONT (MAKE 2 ALIKE)

With size 9 needle, CO 61 (66, 71, 76) sts.

Row 1 (WS): Purl.

Row 2 (RS): Knit.

Rows 3–19 (21, 23, 23): Work even in St st.

Row 20 (22, 24, 24) (RS): K2tog, knit to last 2 sts, K2tog—59 (64, 69, 74) sts rem.

Work 5 rows even.

Work row 20 (22, 24, 24) every 6 rows another 3 times—53 (58, 63, 68) sts rem.

Cont working even in St st to row 53 (53, 59, 59).

Row 54 (54, 60, 60) (RS): K1, M1, knit to last st, M1, K1—55 (60, 65, 70) sts.

Work 5 rows even.

Rep row 54 (54, 60, 60) every 6 rows another 3 times—61 (66, 71, 76) sts.

Cont working even in St st to row 85 (89, 95, 99) or until piece measures 14½ (15, 16, 16½)" from beg. End after completing a WS row.

SHAPE ARMHOLE:

BO 4 (4, 5, 5) sts at beg of next 2 rows—53 (58, 61, 66) sts rem.

Work 2 rows even.

Row 90 (94, 100, 104) (RS): K2tog, knit to last 2 sts, K2tog—51 (56, 59, 64) sts rem.

Work 5 rows even.

Work dec row every 6 rows another 4 (5, 5, 6) times—43 (46, 49, 52) sts rem.

Work 1 more row after last dec row.

BO all sts tightly.

SLEEVES (MAKE 2)

With size 9 needle, CO 44 (46, 48, 50) sts.

Row 1 (WS): Purl.

Row 2 (RS): Knit.

Work in St st for another 17 rows. End after completing a WS row.

Row 20 (RS): K2tog, knit to last 2 sts, K2tog—42 (44, 46, 48) sts rem.

Work 5 rows even.

Work row 20 every 6 rows another 3 times—36 (38, 40, 42) sts rem.

Work even to row 59.

Row 60 (RS): K1, M1, knit to last st, M1, K1—38 (40, 42, 44) sts.

Work 7 rows even.

Work row 60 every 8 rows another 3 (3, 4, 4) times more—44 (46, 50, 52) sts.

Work even until piece measures 18 (18½, 19, 20)" long from beg. End after completing a WS row.

SHAPE TOP SLEEVE:

BO 4 (4, 5, 5) sts at beg of next 2 rows—36 (38, 40, 42) sts rem.

Work 2 rows even.

Next row (RS): K2tog, knit to last 2 sts, K2tog—34 (36, 38, 40) sts rem.

Work 5 rows even.

Work last dec row every 6 rows another 4 (5, 5, 6) times—26 (26, 28, 28) sts rem.

Work 1 more row after last dec row.

BO all sts tightly.

FINISHING

Using mattress st, with purl side facing you, sew side, sleeve, and raglan seams.

Collar: Using 24"-long size 8 circular needle, start at raglan seam with knit side facing you, PU 39 (44, 47, 50) sts on front neck, 24 (24, 26, 28) sts on top sleeve, 39 (44, 47, 50) sts on back neck, and 24 (24, 26, 28) sts on top sleeve—126 (136, 146, 156) sts total. Place marker, join and knit in the round. Work in St st (knit every round) for 10 rounds. Change to 24"-long size 9 circular needle and work for 5 rounds.

Turn.

Next row: Purl across, turn.

Next row: Knit across, turn.

Cont to work back and forth in St st for 3 more rows. Change to 24"-long size 10 circular needle. Work in St st for 10 more rows.

BO with size 10½ needles.

Fold collar down so knit side is facing out.

CROCHET FLOWER

Ch 7, turn.

Row 1: 4 dc in 3rd ch from hook, 4 dc in each of next 4 chs—20 dc, ch 2, turn.

Row 2: 4 dc in each st across—80 dc, ch 2, turn.

Row 3: Rep row 2—320 dc, do not ch 2.

Cut and weave in end.

Thread tapestry needle with a 40"-long piece of yarn and double it so you are sewing with 2 strands of yarn. Turn finished crochet ruffle around like a spiral. Sew up and down and around center until flower is secured. Attach flower in front along opening of collar.

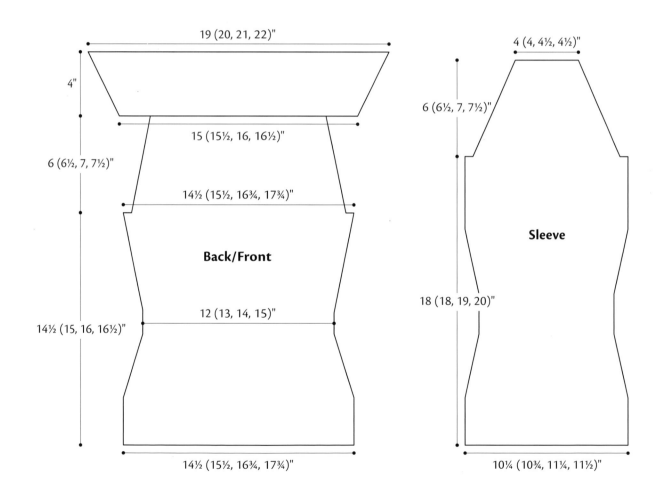

Back/Front

19 (20, 21, 22)"

4"

15 (15½, 16, 16½)"

6 (6½, 7, 7½)"

14½ (15½, 16¾, 17¾)"

12 (13, 14, 15)"

14½ (15, 16, 16½)"

14½ (15½, 16¾, 17¾)"

Sleeve

4 (4, 4½, 4½)"

6 (6½, 7, 7½)"

18 (18, 19, 20)"

10¼ (10¾, 11¼, 11½)"

HONEY SHRUG

The perfect
counterpart to the
Charm Shrug, this
beautiful and cozy
shrug will keep you
warm and stylish.
Combine fine rayon
and wool chenille with
a garter stitch and
ribbing on a circular
needle and you'll
have a masterpiece
in no time.

SIZES

To fit bust: 32–34 (34–36, 36–40)"

Finished width (cuff to cuff): 52 (54, 56)"

SKILL LEVEL: INTERMEDIATE

MATERIALS

MC 12 (14, 15) skeins of Touch Me from Muench Yarns (72% viscose/microfiber, 28% new wool; 1.75 oz/50 g; 61 yds/58 m) in color 3627 (navy blue) [5]

CC 2 (3, 3) skeins of Linie 73 Spot from Online (48% nylon, 40% acrylic, 12% microfiber; 1.75 oz/50 g; 82 yds/75 m) in color 14 (navy and off-white) [5]

2 size 6 circular needles (24" and 40") or size required to obtain gauge

Size 7 circular needle (16") or size required to obtain gauge

Sizes 10 and 10½ needles to BO

Tapestry needle

Clothing label

6 stitch markers (4 green and 2 red, or use the colors of your choice)

GAUGE

18 sts and 38 rows = 4" in garter st on size 7 needle

26 sts and 22 rows = 4" in K2, P2 ribbing patt on size 6 needle

NOTE: Slip the first stitch of every row for a neat, tidy selvage.

SPECIAL STITCHES

Inc: Knit into the front and then into the back of the same stitch

FIRST SLEEVE

WRIST BAND:

With CC and 24"-long size 6 circular needle, CO 54 (58, 62) sts.

Row 1 (WS): *K2, P2*; rep from * to * to last 2 sts, K2.

Row 2 (RS): *P2, K2*; rep from * to * to last 2 sts, P2.

Cont ribbing until piece measures 3" long from beg. End after completing a WS row. Cut yarn and tie on MC. Change to size 7 circular needle.

SHAPE SLEEVE:

Beg working in garter st, inc 1 st at beg and end every 8 rows 7 times—68 (72, 76) sts.

Inc 1 st at beg and end every 6 rows 8 (9, 10) times—84 (90, 96) sts.

BODY

Place a green marker at each end on last inc row.

Work even until piece measures 26 (27, 28)" long from beg. Place a red marker at each end to indicate center section of shrug.

Work even again until garment is equal length from center to green markers. End after completing WS row. Place a green marker at each end as above.

SECOND SLEEVE

SHAPE SECOND SLEEVE:

K2tog at beg and end every 6 rows 8 (9, 10) times—68 (72, 76) sts rem.

K2tog at beg and end every 8 rows 7 times—54 (58, 62) sts rem.

Fold garment in half from center (red marker) to make sure both sleeves are same length (disregarding first wrist-band). Cut yarn and tie on CC.

WRIST BAND:

Rep row 1 and 2 (ribbing) as on first wristband.

Work even in ribbing for 3". BO in patt.

FINISHING

Fold garment in half lengthwise. Using mattress st, sew along seam line from wristband to green markers, secure and weave in ends. Repeat on 2nd sleeve.

TRIM AROUND OPENING:

Using 40"-long size 6 circular needle and CC, join yarn at green marker.

PU 94 (100, 108) sts across top of opening, then PU 114 (124, 132) sts across bottom of opening—208 (224, 240) sts.

Join to work in the round.

Rnd 1: *K2, P2*; rep from * to end.

Cont in ribbing as established for 3¼". BO in patt using size 10 needles for top and size 10½ needles for bottom. Sew in label to indicate top.

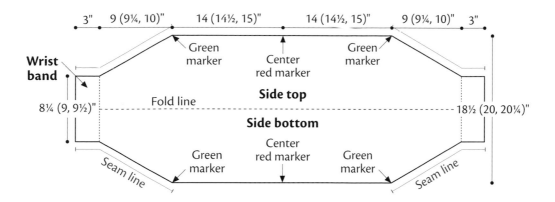

3"   9 (9¼, 10)"   14 (14½, 15)"   14 (14½, 15)"   9 (9¼, 10)"   3"

Green marker

Center red marker

Green marker

Wrist band

Side top

Fold line

8¼ (9, 9½)"

Side bottom

18½ (20, 20¼)"

Green marker

Center red marker

Green marker

Seam line

Seam line

KAREN BAG

Inspired by large baby bags, this structured yet artistic handbag can hide just about anything. Made for on-the-go women, this easy-to-make creation would be a trendsetter in any city.

SIZE

Exact size is based on what yarn you use and the felting process.

Before felting: Approx 23" x 62"

After felting: Approx 11" x 17" x 9"

SKILL LEVEL: INTERMEDIATE

MATERIALS

NOTE: Either Nature Wool or Nature Wool Chunky can be used for this project, giving you more color choices. Both of the yarn weights work well for felting. Nature Wool is thinner, so use 3 strands of yarn held together to knit with. Nature Wool Chunky is thicker, so you only need 2 strands of yarn held together.

MC 7 skeins of Nature Wool from Araucania (100% wool; 3.52 oz/100 g; 240 yds/220 m) in color 01 (off-white)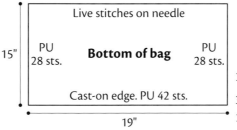

or

MC 8 skeins of Nature Wool Chunky from Araucania (100% wool; 3.52 oz/100 g; 132 yds/120 m) in color 122 (off-white)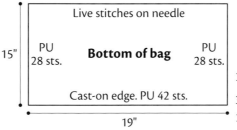

CC1 2 skeins of Cleo from Muench (87% viscose, 13% metal; 1.75 oz/50 g; 62 yds/57 m) in color M381145 (multicolored)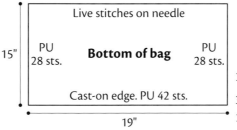

CC2 2 skeins of Flora from Trendsetter Yarns (76% rayon, 24% nylon; .70 oz/20 g; 70 yds/64 m) in color 203 Olive Fiesta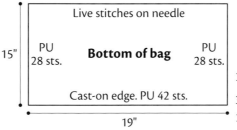

Size 17 circular needle (35") or size required to obtain gauge

Size 10½ needles for button

Size K-10½ (6.5 mm) crochet hook for button

Tapestry needle

Sharp darning needle

One pair of coconut braided purse handles with rings, 26" long

GAUGE

Gauge is not important here. Loose is better than tight. If you knit too tightly, the pieces may not felt properly. Use 2 strands of Nature Wool Chunky or 3 strands of Nature Wool held together to make a swatch.

BOTTOM

Using 2 strands of Nature Wool Chunky or 3 strands of Nature Wool, CO 42 sts with MC. Knit every row for 58 rows. Do not BO.

PU 28 sts on short side, PU 42 sts on long side, and then PU 28 sts on short side—140 sts total. (See diagram below).

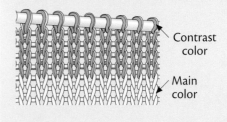

Live stitches on needle

15" | PU 28 sts. | **Bottom of bag** | PU 28 sts.

Cast-on edge. PU 42 sts.

19"

BODY OF BAG

Stripe 1: Knit in the round until piece measures 3" long from PU.

Using the diagram at right as your guide and adding CC yarns as carry-alongs, work stripes as follows:

NOTE: Use 1 less strand of MC on each CC1 stripe. Rather than carry along the nonworking strand, cut it off for each CC1 stripe and add it back in for the next MC stripe.

Stripe 2: Cut 1 strand of MC and add 1 strand of CC1 for 3½".

Stripe 3: MC for 2¼".

Stripe 4: MC and 2 strands of CC2 for 3".

Stripe 5: MC for 2¼".

Stripe 6: Cut 1 strand of MC and add 1 strand of CC1 for 3½".

WORKING WITH TWO YARNS

In order to make the accent color show most effectively, when knitting with the main color and accent color together, be sure the accent yarn stays to the left of the main color yarn on the left needle.

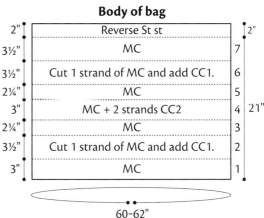

Contrast color

Main color

Stripe 7: MC for 3½".

Piece should measure 21" from PU.

Body of bag

2"	Reverse St st	2"
3½"	MC	7
3½"	Cut 1 strand of MC and add CC1.	6
2¼"	MC	5
3"	MC + 2 strands CC2	4	21"
2¼"	MC	3
3½"	Cut 1 strand of MC and add CC1.	2
3"	MC	1

60-62"

REVERSE STOCKINETTE SECTION:

Next rnd: *P5, P2tog*; rep from * to * for 1 rnd.

Work another 7 rnds in reverse St st (purl every rnd).

BO loosely and cut yarn, leaving an 80" tail for sewing.

FINISHING

Fold top 1" down to the inside and use 2 strands of MC to whipstitch all around. Weave in ends.

Felt according to the instructions on page 76.

SHAPING BAG

Shape, mold, and sculpt your bag until you are happy with it. Fold in gusset at both ends along the top edge of the bag. Measurement between gussets is approximately 14" wide. Stuff bag with tissue paper and cut cardboard to fit bottom of bag. Place cardboard inside to keep shape as bag dries.

ATTACH HANDLES

Thread sharp darning needle with 1 strand of MC and double it so you are sewing with 2 strands of yarn. Place handle on bag using diagram below as guide. Sew in and out from point A to point B. Make sure to secure and weave in tail. Repeat on other side of bag to attach 2nd handle. If you're proficient at sewing, you can line your bag, or add zippered pockets.

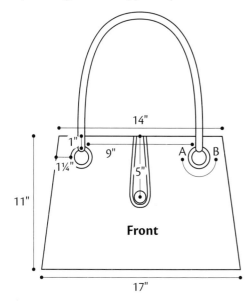

MAKE CLOSURE

BUTTON:

With 1 strand of Nature Wool Chunky or 2 strands of Nature Wool and size 10½ needles, CO 8 sts and leave tail 20" long for sewing. Knit every row until all 4 sides of piece are equal (becomes square). BO all sts. Cut yarn, leaving 30"-long tail.

Thread tail through sharp darning needle as shown.

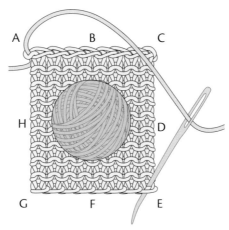

Wind separate strand of yarn into tight ball about 1" in diameter. This will be the inside of button and will show through the knitted square cover, so be creative! (You can use matching or contrasting yarn, or smooth or textured yarn.) Place yarn ball in middle of knitted square and bring the 4 corners to center to wrap yarn ball. Take threaded needle through point A to the opposite corner (point E) and pull tight. Then sew from point C to the opposite corner (point G) and pull tight. Continue closing the loose ends by sewing opposite sides (B to F, D to H) until ball is covered. Be sure to sew covering securely. Use remaining tail of yarn to sew button to front of bag, 5" down from top.

TWISTED CORD:

Cut 4 strands of MC 3½ yds long and 1 strand of CC1 3½ yds long. Combine all 5 strands and knot one end. Attach the knotted end to a door-knob or hook (or ask a friend to help!) and hold the other end fully extended. Begin twisting cord at the end you're holding, continuing to twist until cord is *firm*. Then bring the two ends together, holding center and keeping cord straight to avoid tangling, and allow the two halves of cord to twist together. Tie knot, leaving tails 6" long. Finished cord should be 42" long from knot. Put crochet hook through center of end of cord and draw half of the strands (tail B) through the center of cord, creating a circle.

Fold circle in half by bringing point A to center, and draw tail B through again.

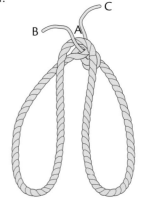

ATTACH CORD ONTO BACK OF BAG:

Attach cord to center of bag between the 2 handles and 4" down from top. With crochet hook, pull tail B and tail C through hole B and hole C ½" apart and tie several knots inside of bag.

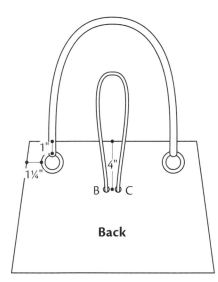

Back

CUDDLE WRAP

This stylish, versatile wrap will warm you up inside and out. Wrap yourself up on a cold day or make it a chic accessory by night by adding an elegant pin.

SIZE

Approx 17" x 80" without fringe

SKILL LEVEL: EASY

MATERIALS

11 skeins of Dune from Trendsetter Yarns (41% mohair, 30% acrylic, 12% viscose, 11% nylon, 6% metal; 1.75 oz/50 g; 90 yds/82 m) in color 100 (variegated) ③

Size 10 circular needle (24") or size required to obtain gauge

Size F-5 (3.75 mm) crochet hook

GAUGE

18 sts = 4" in ribbing patt

NOTE: Slip the first stitch of every row for a neat, tidy selvage. Knit the last stitch through the back loop to help tighten the slipped stitch on the previous row.

DIRECTIONS

CO 76 sts.

Row 1 (WS): Sl 1 kw, *K2, P1*; rep from * to * to last 3 sts, K3.

Row 2 (RS): Sl 1 pw, *P2, K1*; rep from * to * to last 3 sts, P3.

Rep rows 1 and 2 until piece measures 80" in length.

BO tightly in patt.

FINISHING

Cut 96 pieces of yarn for fringe, 20" long. Using 2 strands of yarn for each fringe, attach 24 fringes to each end of wrap with crochet hook.

MYSTIQUE CAPE

Create a sense of mystery or stand out from a crowd of plain black coats. This hooded cape is perfect with a pair of jeans on a cold winter's day.

SIZES

To fit bust: 32–34 (34–36, 36–38, 38–40)"

Finished bust measurements: 38 (40, 42, 44)"

Length: 29 (30, 31, 31)"

SKILL LEVEL: EXPERIENCED

MATERIALS

A 10 (11, 13, 14) skeins of Wave from Filatura di Crosa (75% wool, 25% silk; 1.75 oz/50 g; 126 yds/115 m) in color 12 (brown) ⟨3⟩

B 6 (7, 8, 8) skeins of Gioiello from Filatura di Crosa (30% wool, 30% kid mohair, 20% nylon, 10% cotton, 10% acrylic; 1.75 oz/50 g; 220 yds/200 m) in color 18 (brown) ⟨2⟩

2 size 9 circular needles (32" and 24") or size required to obtain gauge

2 size 8 circular needles (32" and 24") or size required to obtain gauge

Tapestry needle

Cable needle

Six 1" buttons

Sewing needle and matching thread

Stitch markers

GAUGE

17 sts and 24 rows = 4" in St st on size 8 needle with 1 strand of each yarn held tog

20 sts and 21 rows = 4" in ribbing patt on size 9 needle with 1 strand of each yarn held tog

NOTE: Don't work any special selvage stitches. Work the edge stitches in stockinette stitch as for the rest of the row.

SPECIAL STITCHES

C2F (cable 2 front): Sl 2 sts onto cn and leave in front, K2, P2, K2 from cn

Inc: Knit into front and back of same st or purl into front and back of same st to maintain patt

BACK

With A and B held tog and using 32" size 9 needle, CO 162 (174, 186, 198) sts.

Row 1 (WS): *K2, P2*; rep from * to * to last 2 sts, K2.

Row 2 (RS): *P2, K2*; rep from * to * to last 2 sts, P2.

Cont ribbing for 5 more rows.

Row 8 (RS): Work 6 sts, *C2F, work 6 sts*; rep from * to * across.

Work ribbing patt for 3 rows.

Row 12 (RS): Rep row 8.

Work ribbing for 3 rows.

Row 16 (RS): Rep row 8.

Work 1 row. Change to 32" size 8 needle.

Row 18 (RS): Knit and dec 22 (24, 26, 28) sts evenly across—140 (150, 160, 170) sts rem.

Row 19 (WS): P42 (44, 46, 46) sts, pm, P56 (62, 68, 78) sts, pm, purl to end.

Row 20 (RS): Knit to marker, sm, knit to next marker, sm, knit to end.

Work in St st for 3 rows.

Row 24 (RS): Knit to 2 sts before marker, K2tog, sm, knit to next marker, sm, skp, knit to end—138 (148, 158, 168) sts rem.

Work in St st for 3 rows.

Work row 24 every 4 rows another 31 (33, 35, 35) times—76 (82, 88, 98) sts rem. End after completing a WS row.

Next Row (RS): Work row 24 every RS row another 10 times—56 (62, 68, 78) sts rem.

Work 1 WS row even.

SHAPE SHOULDERS:

BO 7 (7, 8, 10) sts at beg of next 4 rows—28 (34, 36, 38) sts rem.

BO all sts loosely.

LEFT FRONT

With A and B held tog, using 24" size 9 needle, CO 78 (90, 102, 114) sts.

Work same as back to row 17. Change to 24" size 8 needle.

Row 18 (RS): Knit, decreasing 5 (12, 19, 26) sts across to last 17 sts, turn and leave remaining 17 sts on st holder for button band—56 (61, 66, 71) sts on needle.

Row 19 (WS): Inc 1 st (purl in front and back of same st), P13 (16, 19, 24), pm, purl to end—57 (62, 67, 72) sts.

Work in St st for another 4 rows.

Row 24 (RS): Knit to 2 st before marker, K2tog, sm, knit to end—56 (61, 66, 71) sts rem.

Work 3 rows even.

Work row 24 every 4 rows another 7 (8, 9, 9) times—49 (53, 57, 62) sts rem.

Work 1 row. End after completing a WS row.

SHAPE ARM OPENING:

Next row (RS): Knit to marker, CO 8 sts for first half; join second ball of A and B for second half, knit to end.

Cont working both halves of front with separate balls of A and B to top of arm opening as follows:

Next row (WS): P12 (15, 18, 23), K3—15 (18, 21, 26) sts in second half; with other ball of A and B, P2, K2, P2, K2, purl to end (first half).

Next row: Knit to 2 sts before marker, K2tog, work ribbing as established to end (first half); with other ball of A and B, knit to end (second half).

Rep last 2 rows, working each side of arm opening with separate balls of yarn, and working K2tog before marker on RS rows as for back until arm opening is 10½ (10½, 11, 11)" from beg. End after completing a RS row.

Next row (WS): Purl across second half, pm, cut yarn leaving a 12"-long tail; BO 8 sts, removing marker when you come to it, replace marker, purl to end. Arm opening has been closed.

Continue working K2tog before marker on RS rows as for back, and working in St st until 19 (22, 25, 30) sts rem, piece should measure approx 27½ (28, 29, 29)" long from CO edge. End after completing a WS row.

SHAPE NECK:

Row 1 (RS): Cont shaping at marker as for back, knit to last 3 sts, K2tog, K1.

Row 2 (WS): Purl.

Work row 1 every RS row another 0 (3, 4, 5) times. Cont to work even at neck edge another 6 (3, 1, 1) rows—14 (14, 16, 20) sts rem. End after completing a WS row.

SHAPE SHOULDER:

Next row (RS): BO loosely 7 (7, 8, 10) sts, knit to end.

Next row (WS): Purl.

BO all sts loosely.

RIGHT FRONT

With A and B held tog, using 24" size 9 needle, CO 78 (90, 102, 114) sts.

Work same as back to row 17. Change to 24" size 8 needle.

Row 18 (RS): Work 17 sts in patt, knit and dec 5 (12, 19, 26) sts evenly across—73 (78, 83, 88) sts rem.

Row 19 (WS): P42 (44, 46, 46), pm, P13 (16, 19, 24), inc 1 st, turn, leave rem 17 sts on st holder—57 (62, 67, 72) sts on needle.

Work in St st for another 4 rows.

Row 24 (RS): Knit to marker, sm, skp, knit to end—56 (61, 66, 71) sts rem.

Work 3 rows even.

Work row 24 every 4 rows another 7 (8, 9, 9) times—49 (53, 57, 62) sts rem. End after completing a RS row.

SHAPE ARM OPENING:

Next row (WS): Purl to marker, CO 8 sts for first half; join second ball of A and B for second half, purl to end.

Continue working both halves of front with separate balls of A and B to top of arm opening as follows:

Next row (RS): Knit across second half; with other ball of A and B, K2, P2, K2, P2, sm, knit to end (first half).

Next row: Purl to second marker, sm, work ribbing as established to end (first half); with other ball of A and B, K3, purl to end (second half).

Next row: Knit across second half; with other ball of A and B, K2, P2, K2, P2, sm, skp, knit to end (first half).

Rep last 2 rows, working each side of arm opening with separate balls of yarn, and working skp after marker on RS rows as for back until arm opening is 10½ (10½, 11, 11)" from beg. End after completing a WS row.

Next row (RS): Knit across second half, pm, cut yarn leaving a 12"-long tail; BO 8 sts, removing marker when you come to it, replace marker, purl to end. Arm opening has been closed.

Cont working skp after marker on RS rows as for back, and working in St st until 19 (22, 25, 30) sts rem, piece should measure the same as left front to neck shaping. End after completing a WS row.

SHAPE NECK:

Row 1 (RS): K1, skp, cont shaping at marker as for back, knit to end.

Row 2 (WS): Purl.

Work row 1 every RS row another 0 (3, 4, 5) times. Cont to work even at neck edge another 7 (4, 2, 2) rows. AT SAME TIME, shape as for back until 14 (14, 16, 20) sts rem. End after completing a WS row.

SHAPE SHOULDER:

Next row (WS): BO loosely 7 (7, 8, 10) sts, purl to end.

Next row (RS): Knit.

BO all sts loosely.

FINISHING

Using mattress st, sew side seams up to shoulders and neck. Using backstitch, sew each end of arm opening.

LEFT FRONT BUTTON BAND

Transfer 17 sts from st holder to 24" size 8 needle. With RS facing you and needle pointing from left to right, rejoin yarns A and B.

Row 1 (RS): Inc in first st, work ribbing to end—18 sts.

Cont ribbing for another 11 (13, 15, 15) rows.

Next row (RS): *† Work 6 sts, C2F, work ribbing patt to end.

Work ribbing patt for 3 rows.

Work last 4 rows another 2 times†.

Work another 10 (12, 14, 14) rows in ribbing*.

Rep cable row from * to * another 4 times.

Rep from † to † once more, then work ribbing for 6 (8, 10, 10) rows.

Put all 18 sts on st holder. Using mattress st, sew button band up along left front.

RIGHT FRONT BUTTON BAND

Transfer 17 sts from st holder to 24"
size 8 needle. With WS facing you
and needle pointing from left to right,
rejoin yarns A and B.

Row 1 (WS): Inc in first st, work
ribbing to end—18 sts.

Cont ribbing for 10 (12, 14, 14) more
rows.

Next row (RS): †Work 6 sts, C2F, work
ribbing to end.

Work ribbing for 3 rows.

Work last 4 rows another 2 times†.

Work another 10 (12, 14, 14) rows of
ribbing. End after completing a WS
row.

BUTTONHOLE:

*Rep from † to †.

Work ribbing another 2 (4, 4, 4) rows.
End after completing a WS row.

Next row (RS): Work 8 sts, BO 2 sts,
work to end.

Next row (WS): Work 8 sts, CO 2 sts,
work to end.

Work ribbing for 6 (6, 8, 8) rows*.

Work from * to * another 3 times.
End after completing a WS row.

Rep from † to †, then work 2 (4, 4, 4)
rows of ribbing.

Next row (RS): Work 8 sts, BO 2 sts,
work to end.

Next row (WS): Work 8 sts, CO 2 sts,
work to end—18 sts.

Do not cut yarn (will be used for
collar later).

Using mattress st, sew button band up
along right front.

Sew on buttons.

COLLAR

Begin at right front where yarns A and
B are still connected.

Row 1 (RS): Work ribbing for 18 sts,
PU 10 (9, 10, 11) sts along right front,
PU 26 (32, 34, 36) sts along back
neck, PU 10 (9, 10, 11) sts along left
front, work ribbing for 18 sts from st
holder—82 (86, 90, 94) sts.

Work even until ribbing measures
3½" long from PU. End after completing a WS row.

Next row (RS): Work 8 sts, BO 2 sts,
work to end—82 (86, 90, 94) sts.

Next row (WS): Work 72 (76, 80, 84)
sts, CO 2 sts, work to end—82 (86,
90, 94) sts.

Work even in ribbing for 4 rows.

If you do not want a hood, BO loosely in
patt.

HOOD

Next row (RS): Work ribbing for 14 sts,
knit until 14 sts rem, work ribbing to end.

Next row (WS): Work ribbing for 14 sts,
purl until 14 sts rem, work ribbing to
end.

Rep last 2 rows until hood measures 5½
(5½, 6, 6)" long. End after completing a
RS row.

Next row (WS): Work ribbing for 14 sts,
P17 (18, 19, 21) sts, pm, P10 (11, 12,
12) sts, pm, P10 (11, 12, 12) sts, pm, P17
(18, 19, 21) sts, work ribbing to end—82
(86, 90, 94) sts.

Next row (RS): Work patt to 2 sts before
first marker, skp, sm, knit to 2 sts before
next marker, skp, sm, K2tog, knit to next
marker, sm, K2tog, work to end—78 (82,
86, 90) sts rem.

Next row (WS): Work ribbing for 14 sts,
purl to last 14 sts, work ribbing to end.

Rep last 2 rows until 3 markers come tog.

BO all sts, cut yarn leaving a 30"-long
tail. Fold hood in half and mattress st
top tog.

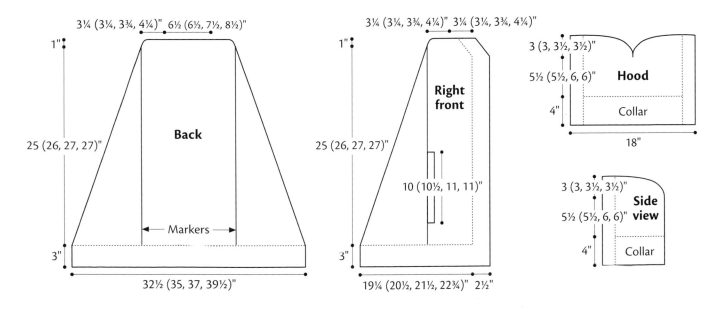

BOYFRIEND SCARF

Make it for him and then steal it often for yourself! This handsome cable design is perfect for men or women. The knitted cashmerino will melt away any frost, and is available in both chunky and Aran weight.

SIZE

Size varies slightly based on which yarn you use. Cables and ribbing draw in, making it difficult to measure precisely.

Cashmerino Chunky: Approx 7" x 72"

Cashmerino Aran: Approx 6" x 68"

SKILL LEVEL: INTERMEDIATE

MATERIALS

7 skeins of Cashmerino Chunky from Debbie Bliss (55% merino wool, 33% microfibre, 12% cashmere; 1.75 oz/50 g; 71 yds/65 m) in color 17017 (red) (4)

or

5 skeins of Cashmerino Aran from Debbie Bliss (55% merino wool, 33% microfibre, 12% cashmere; 1.75 color 003 oz/50 g; 99 yds/90 m) in color 003 (green) (4)

Size 10½ needles for Cashmerino Chunky or size required to obtain gauge

Size 9 needles for Cashmerino Aran or size required to obtain gauge

Cable needle

GAUGE

24 sts = 4" in ribbing patt on size 10½ needles for Cashmerino Chunky

26 sts = 4" in ribbing patt on size 9 needles for Cashmerino Aran

NOTE: Slip the first stitch of every row for a neat, tidy selvage. Knit the last stitch through the back loop to help tighten the slipped stitch on the previous row).

SPECIAL STITCHES

C3F (cable 3 front): Sl 3 sts onto cn and leave in front, K3, P2, K3 from cn

DIRECTIONS

CO 44 sts.

Row 1 (WS): Sl 1 kw, K2, *P3, K2; rep from * to last 3 sts, K3.

Row 2 (RS): Sl 1 pw, P2, *K3, P2; rep from * to last 3 sts, P3.

Row 3 (WS): Rep row 1.

Row 4 (RS): Sl 1 pw, P2, C3F, P2, K3, P2, K3, P2, K3, P2, C3F, P3.

Work ribbing patt for 3 rows.

Row 8 (RS): Rep row 4.

Work ribbing patt for 3 rows.

Row 12 (RS): Rep row 4.

Work ribbing patt for 13 rows.

Row 26 (RS): Sl 1 pw, P2, K3, P2, K3, P2, K3, P2 (18 sts), C3F, work ribbing to end.

Row 27 (and all WS rows through row 37): Work even in ribbing.

Row 28 (RS): Sl 1 pw, P2, K3, P2, K3, P2 (13 sts), C3F, P2, C3F, work ribbing to end.

Row 30 (RS): Rep row 26.

Row 32 (RS): Rep row 28.

Row 34 (RS): Rep row 26.

Row 36 (RS): Rep row 28.

Row 38 (RS): Rep row 26.

Rows 39–51: Work ribbing patt for 13 rows.

Rep rows 4–51 until scarf is 68" long (or desired length).

BO tightly in patt.

This gorgeous green version was knit in Cashmerino Aran.

BOYFRIEND SWEATER

He will love this sweater's soft, roomy feel. She will love its supple, forgiving lines. Share it or not, this sweater is a simple stockinette-stitch pattern that is perfect for anyone.

SIZES

To fit chest: 41–43 (43–45, 45–47)"

Finished chest measurements: 45 (47, 49)"

Sweater length: 27 (28, 29)"

Sleeve length: 25 (26, 27)"

SKILL LEVEL: EASY

MATERIALS

11 (12, 13) skeins of Fashion Trend from Gedifra (51% wool, 49% acrylic; 1.75 oz/50 g; 99 yds/90 m) in color 4512 (self-striping brown and rust) (4)

Size 10 circular needle (24") or size required to obtain gauge

Size 8 circular needle (20")

Size 7 circular needle (20")

Size 10½ needles to BO

Tapestry needle

GAUGE

16 sts and 23 rows = 4" in St st on size 10 needle

NOTE: Don't work any special selvage stitches. Work the edge stitches in stockinette stitch as for the rest of the row.

BACK

With size 10 circular needle, CO 90 (94, 98) sts.

Row 1 (WS): Knit.

Row 2 (RS): Knit.

Work in garter st for 7 more rows. End after completing a WS row.

Row 10 (RS): Knit.

Row 11 (WS): Purl.

Work in St st 86 (88, 90) more rows

or until piece measures 17 (17½, 18)" long.

End after completing a WS row.

SHAPE ARMHOLE:

BO 5 sts at beg of next 2 rows—80 (84, 88) sts rem.

Row 100 (102, 104) (RS): K2, skp, knit until 4 sts rem, K2tog, K2—78 (82, 86) sts rem.

Row 101 (103, 105) (WS): Purl.

Rep last two rows another 24 (25, 26) times—30 (32, 34) sts rem.

BO all sts.

FRONT

With size 10 circular needle, CO 90 (94, 98) sts.

Work same as back to row 101 (103, 105).

Rep row 100 (102, 104) and row 101 (103, 105) another 23 (24, 25) times—32 (34, 36) sts rem.

BO all sts.

RIGHT SLEEVE

With size 10 circular needle, CO 38 (40, 42) sts.

Row 1 (WS): Knit.

Row 2 (RS): Knit.

Work in garter st for 7 more rows. End after completing a WS row.

Row 6 (RS): K2, M1, knit until 2 sts rem, M1, K2—40 (42, 44) sts.

Work even in St st for 5 rows.

Rep last 6 rows another 16 times—72 (74, 76) sts.

Work even to row 119 (125, 131) or until piece measures 21 (22, 23)" long. End after completing a WS row.

SHAPE SLEEVE CAP:

BO 5 sts at beg of next 2 rows—62 (64, 66) sts rem.

Row 122 (128, 134) (RS): K2, skp, knit until 4 sts rem, K2tog, K2.

Row 123 (129, 135) (WS): Purl.

Work last 2 rows another 23 (24, 25) times—14 sts rem. End after completing a WS row.

Next Row (RS): BO 6 sts, K4, K2tog, K2.

Next Row (WS): Purl.

BO all sts.

LEFT SLEEVE

Work the same as right sleeve until 14 sts rem. End after completing a RS row.

Next Row (WS): BO 6 sts, purl to end.

Next Row (RS): K2, skp, knit to end.

BO all sts.

FINISHING

Using mattress st, sew side and sleeve seams. Center side and sleeve seams, sew sleeves in armholes.

ROLL NECK

With size 8 needle, PU 30 (32, 34) sts around front neck, 12 sts around both sleeves, and 28 (30, 32) sts around back neck—82 (86, 90) sts total. Knit in the round for 1". Change to size 7 needle and knit until neck measures 2" from PU.

BO loosely with size 10½ needles.

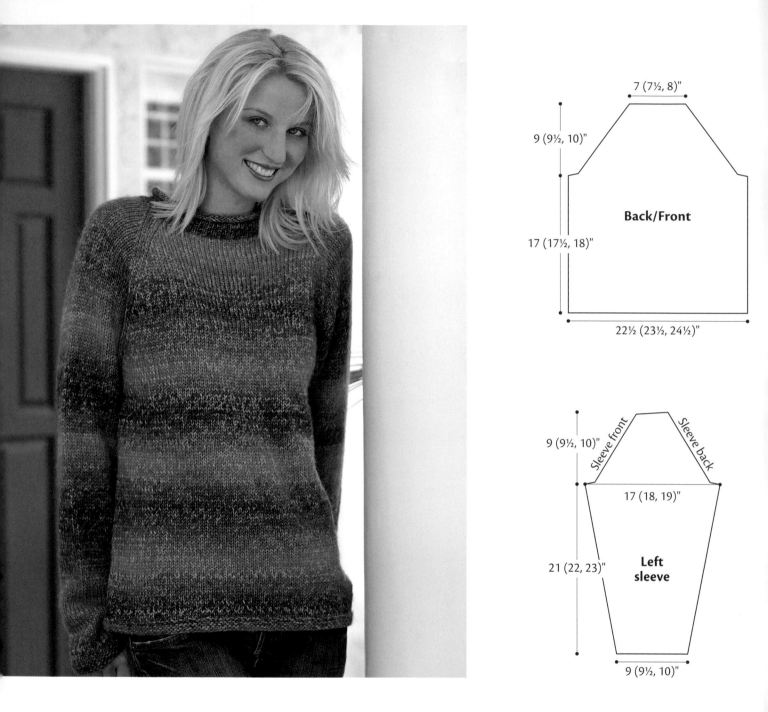

Back/Front

7 (7½, 8)"

9 (9½, 10)"

17 (17½, 18)"

22½ (23½, 24½)"

Left sleeve

Sleeve front

Sleeve back

9 (9½, 10)"

17 (18, 19)"

21 (22, 23)"

9 (9½, 10)"

BABY CAPE

I created this cape 25 years ago as a crocheted item for my daughter and recently updated it as knitwear. It has been a popular gift since its introduction. Kate Hudson, Toby Maguire, and Debra Messing all own one for their children. This wonderful creation is a blanket that doubles as a stylish, functional coat for babies. Pair it with Baby Booties and you'll have a set to pass on for generations.

SIZE

To fit: Newborn–2 years old

Finished measurements: 44" x 26"

SKILL LEVEL: INTERMEDIATE

MATERIALS

MC 8 skeins of Blossom from Trendsetter Yarns (73% nylon, 27% viscose; 1.75 oz/50 g; 92 yds/84 m) in color 15 (yellow) (4)

CC 1 skein of 501 from Filatura di Crosa (100% new wool, 1.75 oz/50 g; 137.5 yds/125 m) in color 218 (red) (3)

Size 10½ circular needle (32") or size required to obtain gauge

Size 9 circular needle (24")

Tapestry needle

4 stitch markers (red, or use the color of your choice)

1 button, ¾"

Sewing needle and matching thread

Approx 2 yds of ribbon, 2"-wide

GAUGE

11 sts = 4" in St st patt on size 10½ needle

NOTE: Slip the first stitch of every row for a neat, tidy selvage.

BODY

With 2 strands of MC held tog on size 10½ needle, CO 120 sts.

Rows 1 (WS) and 2 (RS): Knit.

Work another 4 rows in garter st.

Row 7 (WS): K7, pm, P28, pm, P50, pm, P28, pm, K7.

Row 8 (RS): K7, sm, knit to marker, sm, knit to marker, sm, knit to marker, sm, knit to end.

Row 9 (WS): K7, sm, purl to marker, sm, purl to marker, sm, purl to marker, sm, K7.

Rows 10–15: Work rows 8 and 9 another 3 times.

Row 16 (RS): K7, sm, knit to 2 sts before marker, K2tog, sm, knit to next marker, sm, skp, knit to next marker, sm, K7—118 sts rem.

Work 7 rows in patt as established.

Work rows 16–23 another 7 times—104 sts rem.

Work even until piece measures 17" long from beg. End after completing a WS row.

BUTTON BAND:

Change to size 9 needle and remove all st markers while working next row.

Next row (RS): Sl 1 st, *K2tog*; rep from * to * to last st, K1—53 sts rem. With 2 strands of MC, use thumb CO (see page 74) to CO 20 sts—73 sts total.

Cont knitting with 2 strands of yarn held tog.

Next row (WS): Sl 1 pw, *P1, K1*; rep from * to * to last 2 sts, P2.

Next row (RS): Sl 1 kw, *K1, P1*; rep from * to * to last 2 sts, K2.

Work 1 row in rib patt.

Next row (RS): Work 68 sts in rib patt, YO, K2tog, work to end in patt—73 sts.

Work 2 rows in rib patt, working YO into patt on first row.

Next row (WS): BO 20 sts, work to end—53 sts rem.

SHAPE HOOD

Next row (RS): Knit.

Next row (WS): K7, P39, K7—53 sts.

Rep last 2 rows until hood measures 7".

Knit 3 more rows and BO loosely. Cut yarn, leaving 30"-long tail.

FINISHING

Fold hood in half, place red marker to indicate center.

From each side of red marker, divide by three, place red marker on both sides. (See diagram on page 65.) Using mattress st, sew A to B, cont to C, then cut yarn. Then sew from B to D.

Sew in button on opposite side of buttonhole.

With CC, follow the instructions on page 75 to make 2 pom-poms and attach them to points C and D at top of hood.

Cut ribbon in 4 pieces and tie 4 bows on bottom of cape, using photo as guide.

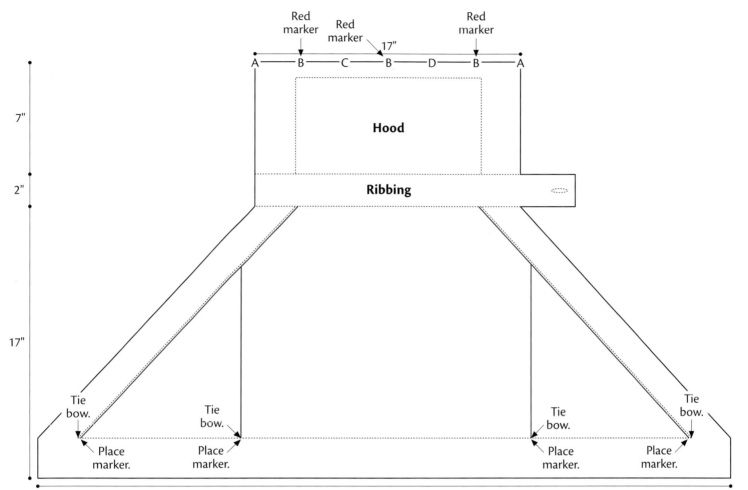

Red
marker

Red
marker

Red
marker

17"

A —— B —— C —— B —— D —— B —— A

7"

Hood

2"

Ribbing

17"

Tie
bow.

Tie
bow.

Tie
bow.

Tie
bow.

Place
marker.

Place
marker.

Place
marker.

Place
marker.

44"

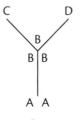

C   D

B

B   B

A   A

Hood seams

BABY BOOTIES

When shoes are just
too uncomfortable,
these booties cover
up cold little toes
fashionably. Made
using simple knit
techniques, these
booties make a
thoughtful baby gift.

SIZES

To fit: 3–6 months

Height: 3½" from bottom of bootie

SKILL LEVEL: INTERMEDIATE

MATERIALS

MC 1 skein (or yarn left over from Baby Cape on page 63) of Blossom from Trendsetter Yarns (73% nylon, 27% viscose; 1.75 oz/50 g; 92 yds/84 m) in color 15 (yellow) 🔲4

CC 1 skein of 501 from Filatura di Crosa (100% new wool; 1.75 oz/50 g; 137.5 yds/125 m) in color 218 (red) for pom-pom 🔲3

Size 7 needles or size required to obtain gauge

Size C-2 (2.75 mm) crochet hook for attaching pom-poms

Tapestry needle

GAUGE

20 sts = 4" in garter st on size 7 needles

DIRECTIONS

With MC, CO 31 sts.

Row 1 (WS): K15, inc (knit in front and back of same st), K15—32 sts.

Rows 2, 4, and 6 (RS): Knit.

Row 3: K15, inc, inc, K15—34 sts.

Row 5: K15, inc, K2, inc, K15—36 sts.

Row 7: K15, inc, K4, inc, K15—38 sts.

Row 8 (RS): K23, K2tog tbl, turn.

SHAPE FOOT:

Next row (WS): Sl 1 pw, K8, P2tog, turn.

Next row (RS): Sl 1 kw, K8, K2tog tbl, turn.

Work last 2 rows another 4 times.

Next row (WS): Sl 1 pw, K8, P2tog, K8—26 sts rem.

SHAPE ANKLE:

Next row (RS): *(K2, P2)*, rep from * to * to last 2 sts, K2.

Next row (WS): *(P2, K2)*, rep from * to * to last 2 sts, P2.

Work last 2 rows another 2 times.

Next 6 rows: Knit.

BO loosely.

FINISHING

Using mattress st, sew back and sole seams.

MAKE POM-POMS AND TIES:

Cut 70"-long strand of CC and make first pom-pom on one end (following instructions on page 75) and leave long tail to crochet. Using crochet hook, ch for 14", leaving 6"-long tail to tie on second pom-pom. *Do not make second pom-pom until after you weave first pom-pom into baby bootie.* With tail of first pom-pom and beginning at front center of baby bootie, weave in and out, ¾" apart. Now that you are back at front center of baby bootie, make second pom-pom and tie it onto other end of crochet ch.

Repeat on 2nd bootie.

Hazel Bag

There is no better way to welcome spring than with a flash of this sassy not-too-big, not-too-small purse. Made on a circular needle with a knit stitch, this creation is irresistible eye candy.

SIZE

Exact size is based on what yarn you use and the felting process.

Before felting: Approx 16" x 14" or 14" x 13"

After felting: Approx 10" x 7"

SKILL LEVEL: EASY

MATERIALS

Note: Either Nature Wool or Nature Wool Chunky can be used for this project, giving you more color choices. Both of the yarn weights work well for felting. Nature Wool is thinner, so use 3 strands of yarn held together to knit with. Nature Wool Chunky is thicker, so you only need 2 strands of yarn held together.

MC 3 skeins of Nature Wool from Araucania (100% wool; 3.52 oz/100 g; 240 yds/220 m) in color 42 (pink) (4)

or

MC 3 skeins of Nature Wool Chunky from Araucania (100% wool; 3.52 oz/100 g; 132 yds/120m) in color 22 (pink) (5)

CC 1 skein of Linie 85 Smash from Online (100% polyester; 1.75 oz/50 g; 99 yds/90 m) in color 0017 (pink) (3)

Size 17 circular needle (26") or size required to obtain gauge

Tapestry needle

Sharp darning needle

One pair of plastic, translucent pink purse handles, 6" long

3 purchased silk flowers in different sizes (or make your own flowers following the instructions on page 70)

Scrubbing brush

GAUGE

Gauge is not important here. Loose is better than tight. If you knit too tightly, the pieces may not felt properly. Use 2 strands of Nature Wool Chunky or 3 strands of Nature Wool held tog to make swatch.

BOTTOM

Using 2 strands of Nature Wool Chunky or 3 strands of Nature Wool held tog, CO on 18 sts with MC.

Knit every row for 28 rows. Do not BO.

PU 18 sts for each side—72 sts total. (See diagram.)

BODY OF BAG:

Knit in the round until piece measures 12" long from PU. (See diagram for exceptions.) Cut 1 strand of MC and add 1 strand of CC and work in the round until piece measures 2" long from adding CC.

BO loosely.

FINISHING

Fold top 1" down to inside and use 2 strands of MC to whipstitch all around. Weave in ends. Use scrubbing brush to brush out CC section until it is full of long eyelash.

Felt according to instructions on page 76.

SHAPING BAG

Shape, mold, and sculpt your bag until you are happy with it. Stuff bag with tissue paper to hold the shape as it dries.

ATTACH HANDLES

Thread sharp darning needle with 1 strand of MC and double it. Place handle on bag using diagram as guide. Sew in and out from point A to point B. Make sure to secure and weave in tail. Repeat on other side of bag to attach 2nd handle. Sew on flowers.

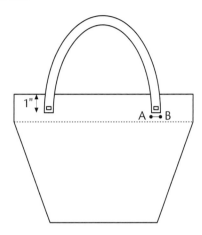

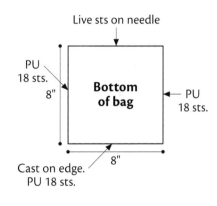

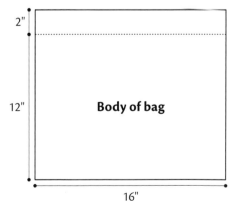

FELTED FLOWERS

These fun flowers
are used on several
of the projects in this
book, and can also
be made as separate
pieces of jewelry or
as embellishments for
other knitting
projects.

SIZE

Felting is an art, not a science, and each yarn and color will felt to a different size. Because these flowers are not made to fit like a garment, and because real flowers and leaves come in a variety of shapes and sizes, I have not listed any exact dimensions here, although I do include instructions for making big, medium, and small pieces.

SKILL LEVEL: INTERMEDIATE

MATERIALS

Flowers can be made using the yarn I list below, or with any yarn that you have in your stash that will felt. Animal fibers such as 100% wool or a blend of wool and mohair are excellent choices. Machine-washable wool (sometimes labeled "super-wash"), cotton, silk, and man-made fibers will not felt.

Flowers: 3 skeins of Nature Wool from Araucania (100% wool; 3.52 oz/100 g; 240 yds/220 m) in 3 different colors of your choice (4)

Leaves: 1 skein of Nature Wool from Araucania (100% wool; 3.52 oz/100 g; 240 yds/220 m) in color 27 (green) (4)

Size 10 needles

Tapestry needle

Sharp darning needle

Polyester sewing thread to match colors of flowers and leaves

Sewing needle

GAUGE

Gauge is not important here. Loose is better than tight. If you knit too tightly, the pieces may not felt properly.

MAKING THE FLOWERS
Big Flowers

CENTER PETALS:

(Make 2 in same color for each flower.)

CO 13 sts

Work even in St st for 3", then dec every 2" on one side until 4 or 5 sts rem. BO.

OUTER PETALS:

(Make 4 in same color for each flower.)

CO 10 sts.

Work in St st for 4". BO.

Medium Flowers
CENTER PETAL:

CO 12 sts.

Work in St st and AT THE SAME TIME dec every 1" on one side until 4 or 5 sts rem. BO.

Small Flowers
CENTER PETAL:

CO 10 sts.

Work in St st and AT THE SAME TIME dec every 1" on one side until 4 or 5 sts rem. BO.

MAKING THE LEAVES

Big Leaf

CO 11 sts.

Work in St st for 2½", then dec 1 st on each end every 6 rows until 3 or 4 sts rem. BO.

Medium Leaf

CO 9 sts.

Work in St st for 1", then dec 1 st on each end every 4 rows until 3 or 4 sts rem. BO.

Small Leaf

CO 12 sts.

Work in St st for 4". BO.

Extra-Small Leaf

CO 10 sts.

Work in St st for 3". BO.

FELTING

Place pieces in a zippered pillow-case and put in washing machine (wash different colors separately). Set machine to hot wash and cold rinse cycles, and wash on small load for 15 minutes. Do not let machine go into rinse or spin cycles. Pieces do not have to be thick, but knitting should be matted.

SHAPING AFTER FELTING:

Pull small or extra-small leaves diagonally and pull petals, big leaves, and medium leaves horizontally to stretch them out flat. Finish shaping as follows:

Leaves. Form into leaf shape with a little curve or twist to look natural; clip leaves with pin or clamp and let dry.

Petals. Starting with pointy tip of felted piece (curled side away from you), roll into shape of bud or rose; clip flower with pin or clamp and let dry.

SEWING THE FLOWERS

These flowers are intended to be free-style design; imperfection is expected since flowers are not all the same in nature. When creating flowers, you'll get the best results when you instill your own personality and creativity. Remember, Mother Nature's flowers are all unique, and yours should be too. Just have fun!

CENTER PETAL:

Using color thread that matches petals, thread sewing needle with 4 strands of thread, 36" long. With knit side facing you, begin at narrow end of petal, fold petal in ½"; whipstitch at base of petal and secure tightly.

At start of rolling, knit side will be the inside of petals and purl side will be the outside, but this will change later on. Continue rolling petal and whipstitch to secure. Try to roll so that top of petal flares out and bottom looks like a cone.

Approximately a third of the way, twist unrolled portion of petal so wrong side (purl side) is facing you, continue to roll petal and whipstitch to secure.

The amount of twisting and turning is up to you, depending on length of petal and how you want your flower to look. Although you need to secure base of flower tightly, be sure to keep top of petal loose and wavy like a rose.

The purpose of twisting petal from right side to wrong side and back is to break the continuous line so that flower looks more natural. Continue to twist and whipstitch to secure base until you run out of petal. If you run out of thread, rethread with 4 strands and continue.

When at end of flower, sew up and down between petals (between creases). This is so stitching will not be obvious. Remember to leave top of petals loose. This process completes a medium-sized flower.

OUTER PETALS:

To create a larger flower, add more petals on the sides. The more petals added, the larger the flower. Be sure to secure the stitches tightly each time at base of flower.

ATTACH LEAVES:

Starting with medium leaf, with purl side facing you, make crease at larger end so piece will look like a leaf. Place leaf under flower and whipstitch end of leaf to base of flower to secure. Then place flower and leaf on knitted item and secure from back side of item to middle of flower. Take small leaf and cut diagonally; then bend the piece in the middle to create 2 small leaves. Don't be afraid to cut leaves; felting keeps stitches from fraying. Place small leaves under flower and secure to item and flower. The larger leaves should be bent with tip secured to bag. Leave small leaves loose. Attach as many leaves as you like. This is a freestyle flower design; each flower should have its own unique personality.

For the arrangement I used on the Julia Bag (at right and on page 34), make 3 different-sized flowers and approximately 11 leaves. For the arrangement on the Hazel Bag (page 68), make 3 small- or medium-sized flowers and approximately 7 small and extra-small leaves. The color and placement of the flowers is up to your creative design. Secure flowers and leaves to bag, being sure to secure very well inside bag before cutting thread. If you choose to line your project, lining will cover your stitches on inside of bag.

Remember, be creative and have fun!

Knitting is a wonderful hobby—fun, creative, and relaxing. I love the excitement of starting a new project, choosing my favorite yarn, and imagining how beautiful the finished item will be. But the finishing touches on a project are just as important as the colors and fibers you choose. My wish is for you to enjoy the process, and wear the finished garment proudly!

TIPS AND TRICKS

Here are some of my favorite tips and tricks for smooth knitting and professional-looking results.

Gauge

It's very important to check your gauge before every project you begin. To make a gauge swatch, use the stitch pattern and needles recommended for the project. Cast on about 20 to 24 stitches and work until your swatch measures 5". Bind off loosely.

To measure the stitch gauge, place a ruler or tape measure across your swatch horizontally. Mark the beginning and end of 4" (10 cm) with pins and count the stitches between the pins.

To measure the row gauge, place a ruler or tape measure across your swatch vertically. Mark the beginning and end of 4" (10 cm) with pins and count the stitches between the pins.

Tying on Yarn

Start a new ball of yarn on the edge of the project and never in the middle. Remember to leave a tail 4" to 6" long that you can later weave in with a tapestry needle.

Thumb Cast On

The thumb cast on is sometimes called the "e" cast on or the backwards loop cast on. It is worked with one knitting needle. This is a good way to add stitches at the end of a row.

1. Make a slipknot and put it on the needle.

2. Holding the needle in your right hand, make a loop around the thumb of your left hand.

3. Insert the needle into the loop on your thumb and pull your thumb out of the loop, tightening it on the needle.

Repeat steps 2 and 3 until the desired number of stitches have been cast on.

Slip Stitch

Slipping the first stitch of every row when knitting a scarf or shawl will improve the look of the edge of your project, especially when doing garter stitch and binding off. You will notice in my instructions that I advise you when to slip the first stitch.

Knit through the Back Loop

Knit the last stitch through the back loop; this will help tighten the slipped stitch on the previous row. This only applies on ribbing or stockinette stitch, where the pattern requires slipping the first stitch of a row and there is a knit stitch at the end of the row.

Pressing

With the wrong side of your knitted pieces facing up, pin each piece onto an ironing board and shape it to the measurement that was given. Set your iron to the temperature according to the yarn label, layer a cotton sheet over the piece, and press. Pressing your projects will help even out your stitches, maintain the project's shape, and give a smooth finish.

Picking up Stitches

To pick up stitches on a cast-on or bind-off edge, go into each stitch along the edge and pick up one new stitch.

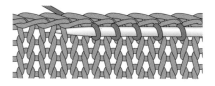

To pick up stitches along the side of a piece of knitting, pick up one stitch between each row of knitting.

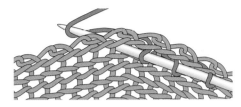

Making Pom-poms

Cut a piece of yarn 25" long and place it between your index and middle fingers, with the center of the strand folding over your middle finger as shown (strand A). Open your index finger and middle finger to the size of the pompom you want. Take another strand of yarn (strand B) and wrap it around the two fingers (closer to the tips of the fingers) for a total of 30 rounds. The more you wrap, the fuller the finished pom-pom.

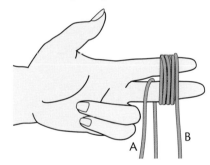

Cut the yarn (strand B). Now take the two ends of strand A and tie a knot around the middle of the loops created by strand B.

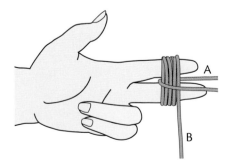

Take the pom-pom off your fingers and tie a second firm knot; then tie a third firm knot to secure. Cut the loops on both sides of the knot. Trim the pompom until it's an even round ball. Shake the pom-pom to remove excess yarn or fuzz.

Making Fringe

Cut strands of yarn a little longer than double the length of the fringe you want. Fold each strand in half to make a loop on one end. Insert a crochet hook from the front to the back of the end of the scarf or shawl and pull the loop through. Then use the crochet hook to pull the tails tightly through each loop.

Garter Stitch

Back and forth: Knit every row.

Circular: Knit one round, purl one round.

Stockinette Stitch

Back and forth: Knit one row, purl one row.

Circular: Knit every round.

SEWING SEAMS

These are the seaming techniques that I use to create professional results.

Mattress Stitch

The mattress stitch creates an invisible seam. Here are a few tips:

• Work the stitch with the right side always facing you; this way the seam will be on the inside of the piece

• The tapestry needle is always parallel to the edges when picking up a bar

• Work one stitch in from the edge

• After casting on or binding off, always leave an extra-long tail for sewing seams

To get started, thread a needle with the yarn tail that is attached to the project. If you do not have a yarn tail long enough, then attach a new piece of yarn. Insert the needle from the front (right side) to the back (wrong side) in the corner opposite the yarn tail, and then up from the wrong side to the right side. Pull tight to close the gap.

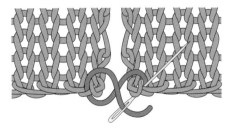

Insert the needle down and pick up one or two bars depending on the yarn weight (if the yarn is bulky, pick up 1 bar; if it's thin, pick up 2 bars) from the opposite side of where the yarn is attached. Pull the yarn through and insert the needle into the corresponding bar on the opposite side. Continue to work back and forth.

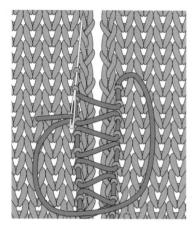

If you choose to have the piece's wrong side be the right side, work as above, but with the wrong side facing you.

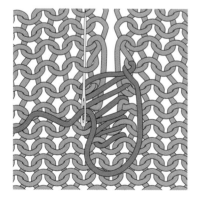

Backstitch

A backstitch seam is often used to secure the ends of sewing or add casing to purses or bikinis.

To begin the seam, take the needle around the edge of the knitting twice, from back to front. *Insert the needle into the same spot where the yarn came out from the previous stitch; then bring the needle back up to the front of the knitting about two stitches or rows to the left, and pull through. Repeat from * until the entire seam is sewn.

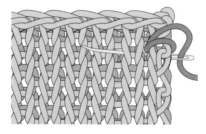

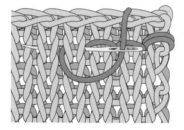

Whipstitch

With the right or wrong sides of the fabric facing up as instructed in the pattern, place the two pieces to be seamed on a flat surface. Thread a tapestry needle with matching yarn or thread. Catch the stitch on the edge of one piece of knitting and then catch a stitch on the other piece. Continue to sew along the seam, pulling the yarn gently after each stitch to close the seam.

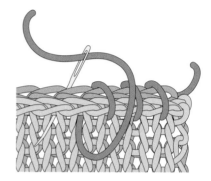

FELTING

Put the item in the washing machine. Set your washing machine for a small cycle on hot. Turn the machine on and let it agitate. The combination of hot water and agitation will help the felting process. Stop the washing machine and check your item every 5 or 10 minutes; straighten and pull the item in every direction, making sure there are no wrinkles or unevenness. Don't let the machine go into the rinse or spin cycle; this will deform your item. Continue washing and shaping your bag until the fabric is firm and the desired size is achieved. Before draining your washing machine; be sure to clean your water with a strainer to catch all the fuzz that could clog your machine. Place the item between two dry towels on the floor and step on it to squeeze out any excess water. See the shaping instructions for each individual project.

CROCHET FINISHING TECHNIQUES

Here are instructions for the crochet techniques I use for finishing projects.

Chain Stitch (ch)

Place a slipknot on the crochet hook. Wrap the yarn around the hook, and then pull the working yarn through the loop on the hook, forming a new loop.

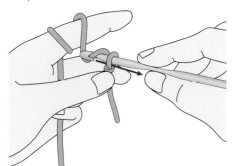

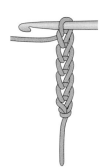

Repeat until the required number of stitches has been created.

Single Crochet (sc)

Single crochet makes a smooth edge on a knitted piece. Working from right to left, insert the hook into the next stitch on the edge of the knitted piece, yarn over, and pull the working yarn through the loop from the stitch.

Two loops are now on the hook. Yarn over, and then pull the working yarn through both loops on the hook.

One loop remains on the hook. You are ready for the next stitch.

Half Double Crochet (hdc)

This stitch is slightly taller than single crochet, and also makes a nice finish on a knitted piece. Yarn over and insert the hook into the next stitch. Pull the yarn through the stitch.

There are three loops on the hook. Yarn over, and then pull the working yarn through all three loops on the hook.

One loop remains on the hook. You are ready for the next stitch.

Double Crochet (dc)

This is a tall stitch that I often use to crochet flowers (such as the flower on Passion Sweater on page 42). Yarn over and insert the hook into the next stitch. Yarn over and pull the yarn through the stitch. There are three loops on the hook. Yarn over, and then pull the working yarn through two loops on the hook; two loops remain on the hook.

Yarn over, and then pull the working yarn through two loops on the hook.

One loop remains on the hook. You are ready for the next stitch.

approx	approximately
beg	begin(ning)
BO	bind off
CC	contrasting color
ch	chain or chain stitch
cn	cable needle(s)
CO	cast on
cont	continue(ing)
dc	double crochet
dec	decrease(ing)
g	gram
hdc	half double crochet
inc	increase(ing)
k	knit
k2tog	knit 2 stitches together—1 stitch decreased
kw	knitwise
lp	loop
MC	main color
M1	make 1 stitch
oz	ounce(s)
p	purl
p2tog	purl 2 stitches together—1 stitch decreased
patt	pattern
pm	place marker
PU	pick up and knit
pw	purlwise
rem	remain(ing)
rep	repeat
rev St st	reverse stockinette stitch
RS	right side
rnd	round
sc	single crochet
skp	slip 1 knitwise, knit 1, pass slipped stitch over—1 stitch decreased
sl	slip
sl st	slip stitch(es)—slip stitches purlwise unless instructed otherwise
sm	slip marker
st(s)	stitch(es)
St st	stockinette stitch
tbl	through back loop(s)
tog	together
WS	wrong side
yd(s)	yard(s)
YO	yarn over

HELPFUL TABLES

METRIC CONVERSIONS			
m	=	yds	x	0.9144
yds	=	m	x	1.0936
g	=	oz	x	28.35
oz	=	g	x	0.0352

KNITTING NEEDLE SIZES

Millimeter Range	U.S. Size Range
2.25 mm	1
2.75 mm	2
3.25 mm	3
3.5 mm	4
3.75 mm	5
4 mm	6
4.5 mm	7
5 mm	8
5.5 mm	9
6 mm	10
6.5 mm	10½
7 mm	10¾
8 mm	11
9 mm	13
10 mm	15
12.75 mm	17
15 mm	19
19 mm	35
25 mm	50

SKILL LEVELS

Beginner: Projects for first-time knitters using basic knit and purl stitches. Minimal shaping.

Easy: Projects using basic stitches, repetitive stitch patterns, and simple color changes. Simple shaping and finishing.

Intermediate: Projects using a variety of stitches, such as basic cables and lace, simple intarsia, and techniques for double-pointed needles and knitting in the round. Midlevel shaping and finishing.

Experienced: Projects using advanced techniques and stitches, such as short rows, Fair Isle, more intricate intarsia, cables, lace patterns, and numerous color changes.

YARN WEIGHTS

STANDARD YARN-WEIGHT SYSTEM

Yarn-Weight Categories and Symbols	Super Fine (1)	Fine (2)	Light (3)	Medium (4)	Bulky (5)	Super Bulky (6)
Types of Yarn in Category	Sock, Fingering, Baby	Sport, Baby	DK, Light Worsted	Worsted, Afghan, Aran	Chunky, Craft, Rug	Bulky, Roving
Knit Gauge Ranges in Stockinette Stitch to 4"	27 to 32 sts	23 to 26 sts	21 to 24 sts	16 to 20 sts	12 to 15 sts	6 to 11 sts
Recommended Needle in Metric Size Range	2.25 to 3.25 mm	3.25 to 3.75 mm	3.75 to 4.5 mm	4.5 to 5.5 mm	5.5 to 8 mm	8 mm and larger
Recommended Needle in U.S. Size Range	1 to 3	3 to 5	5 to 7	7 to 9	9 to 11	11 and larger

Quick Thinking and Cleverness

What differentiates My Phuong, my mother, from others is her ability to find quick, clever solutions to challenges. This is true both professionally and personally. Fifteen years ago, our family had its first American-style turkey for Thanksgiving. My Phuong had to work the day before and asked my father to clean the turkey. While at work, she learned that my father had cleaned the turkey so well that even the skin was removed. With the same skills that helped her survive all those years of war in Vietnam and in impoverished refugee camps, she creatively sewed the turkey's skin back on. Our first American turkey dinner was a delicious "Frankenturkey." My Phuong employs the same quick thinking and cleverness for her clients. Whether it's a sweater too short for a son who has unexpectedly grown 4" or a simple stitch dropped five rows ago, she rescues with ease. This is knit couture, My Phuong–style.
—*Brenda Huynh*

Meet My Phuong

My Phuong (she prefers to be addressed by her middle and first name together) emigrated from Vietnam in 1980 when the aftermath of the Vietnam War took its toll on her family. Throughout her life and the three years her family spent in impoverished refugee camps, she never ceased knitting or passing on her knowledge of the craft. Both of her daughters are knitters, and the younger, Brenda, is her partner and codesigner at Knitport. My Phuong has always been an artist—designing her home, designing hair as a hairdresser to help her husband put their children through college, painting, drawing, sewing, embroidering, sculpting, and of course knitting. Each finished product—whether sewn, knitted, sculpted, or painted—exhibits her artistry.

My Phuong learned to knit and crochet when she was six years old. She has been teaching the skills of knitting for 20 years, most recently in organized classes at her boutique, Knitport. She designs approximately two pieces per month and writes her own patterns. Almost 100% of the designs displayed at Knitport are My Phuong originals.